Praise for BRANDED YOU

From the very beginning of this book I felt such a sense of relief and anticipation. This book is so timely and important for entrepreneurs and leaders who are passionate about making a difference. Adèle brings her strengths to empower readers with creativity, engaging ideas and powerful questions. This is one of those books that will travel the world, underlined, pages tagged, and inspiring radical, brave personal branding that changes lives. Well done Adèle, and thank you!

— **Kerrie Phipps**, International Speaker, Author: *Do Talk To Strangers: How To Connect With Anyone, Anywhere*
www.kerriephipps.com

From social media tips to a free ebook and networking advice, Adèle McLay has successfully created a book packed full of useful, practical ways to develop and enhance your personal brand. Written in the informal, engaging tone that Adèle delivers so well, this is a must-have for anyone looking to take their business to the next level.

— **Jessica Fabrizi**, Founder of One Degree To Connect
www.onedegreetoconnect.com

Like most busy, successful entrepreneurs, I have very little time to invest in things that don't make a big difference. If I'm going to spend time learning any new skill or information, it needs to be spot-on, creative, and actionable right now. Branded You has absolutely exceeded those expectations. Adèle has taken her decades of knowledge and experience to create a completely new and impactful approach to branding the single most important asset in your business...you.

— **Dallas Hardcastle**, Business Growth Specialist
www.dallashardcastle.com

How I wish this book had been available when I first started my business consultancy practice. Whilst I was familiar with building a company brand, personal branding was completely new to me. I got HUGE value from this book. It's honest, straight-talking and is relevant, whether you're starting out in business or a more experienced platform builder. I loved the interactive sections where Adèle poses pertinent questions to help the reader think through their personal branding strategies. Adèle's personal brand star system™' is inspired and I have it pinned up to keep me focused! This book will be an invaluable resource for years to come.

— **Denyse Whillier**, Founder of Built To Succeed™ & Business Champions
www.denysewhillier.com

Having recently met Adèle McLay who spoke passionately at a business networking event focussing on Personal Branding, I have been eagerly awaiting the release of her latest oeuvre 'Branded You'. Adèle has taken me on an insightful journey, challenging me throughout to identify and hone in on my market niche; whilst remaining authentic and true to the heart of my vision. This is definitely not a 'passive' read, Adèle is an engaging author, making you work hard as her book is packed full of useful exercises to apply what you read to your own career and personal branding. As a small business owner, this book has reignited my passion, and I look forward to putting into practise the insights shared to refocus my career as 'Branded Me'.

— **Virginia Van West,** Freelance Business Services
www.virginiavanwest.com

As a business academic in a previous life, and a small business owner previously in New Zealand and now Australia, I enjoyed reading Adèle's 'Branded You' book. It is empowering and inspiring, and most of all grounded in practice. Adèle's experience and expertise have enabled her to bring together 'what we do' and 'who we are' to shape our own personal brand. Adèle backs up her framework/model with interesting examples and case studies, including sharing her own business issues. She takes you on a journey which is easy to read and identify with, and includes actions to take on your own business, now or in the future. I certainly identified with areas that I can improve on, and will make those priorities going forward.

— **Dr Linda Turner**, Founder BizExpanz
www.bizexpanz.com

When it comes to BRANDING, there's no one on the planet BOLDER and BRAVER than Adèle McLay. Within the pages of this book, Adèle teaches the priceless lesson of 7+1 Pillars of Personal Brand Success — and for your sake, I hope you read each word, dog-ear the corners, highlight passages, and then apply what you learn... because what she shares can change your life!   You are 'Branding Yourself' everyday; I'd recommend that you do it the Adèle McLay way.

— **Duane Cummings**, Co-Founder, The Speakers Guild of America; Founder, The Sensational Group LLC; Author: *The Sensational Salesman*

www.duanecummings.com

BRANDED
YOU

HOW TO STAND OUT IN BUSINESS AND
ACHIEVE GREATER PROFITABILITY AND SUCCESS

Adèle McLay

Akitu

AKITU PRESS
London, United Kingdom

First Edition published 2016.

Akitu Press Limited, P O Box 56429, London SE3 9UF.

British Library Cataloguing in Publication Data.

McLay, Adèle.
Branded You: How to stand out in business, and achieve greater profitability and success
Copyright © 2016 by Adèle McLay. All rights reserved.
A catalogue record for this book is available from the British Library.
Paperback Edition ISBN: 978-0-9926916-2-2
Digital Edition ISBN: 978-0-9926916-3-9

Photography by Jonathan Jacob – jjacobphotography.co.uk

Book Design by Lucie Mauger – www.luciemauger.co.uk

To business owners and entrepreneurs across the world who work hard year in and year out making a difference in the lives of their customers. This book is for you.

Be bold. Be brave. Be branded.

Contents

Acknowledgements

Writing a book involves team work. I am especially grateful to the small and highly focused team that has supported me in writing and publishing this book.

To Kate Adams, my editor extraordinaire, thank you for your patience and guidance as this book got written and rewritten. You are exceptional at what you do and your knowledge and insights have been invaluable.

To Nicola Wilkinson, my long serving personal assistant, thank you for getting on with your 'day job' while I locked myself away for long periods on this book, and for your ongoing proofreading and editing.

To Lucy Sheehan and Helen de Beresford, my marketing team, thank you for all your work and contributions to the book.

To Lucie Mauger, my graphic designer and typesetter, thank you for working with me again. This is our second book project together and I look forward to working on others with you.

To all the public figures and business owners who have inspired me with the way in which they've developed their personal brands, thank you. Without you this book wouldn't have been written.

Finally, a big thank you to my family. David, my greatest (and most patient) supporter, thank you for keeping the home fires burning while I toil over my work. To Alex, my stepson, thank you for your ongoing interest in my work. I hope in some way this book inspires and guides you in your own career. To Gemma, our young teenage daughter, thank you sweetie for understanding that my work is very important to me. I love you all very much.

PART 1: Our New World

The world as each of us knows it and relates to it has changed radically in the past few years. When it comes to standing out and being noticed, in whatever it is that we do, technology has gone a long way towards levelling the playing field. This is exciting because new opportunities are opening up, while in other ways it can be overwhelming when there appears to be so many people clamouring for a finite amount of attention.

The answer is personal branding. Take a look at any of the successful people in your niche or more generally whom you admire. What do they stand for, what do they represent? Chances are you won't have to think long for the answer because their personal brand is crystal clear and out there for everyone to see, everyone who matters that is. Why do people think of them as the 'go to' person in their niche, the thought leader, the memorable person, the power connector? What is it that they offer? Why do they stand out?

These are the people who have their personal brand nailed. And simply put, that means their purpose, their values, their personality, their pitch and the people they serve/entertain/help/inspire are in complete alignment. They elicit an emotional response that creates first a connection, then a relationship, loyalty, support, backing and even love. 'I love that guy'. 'Isn't she the best?' 'You must call him'.

It doesn't matter what kind of work you do. It's your personal brand that will give you the edge over the competition, build your network and have people coming to you with opportunities because you're the person they trust, like and admire. You know what promise you can offer, you communicate that promise and you deliver on it. That's the power of personal branding.

****

Imagine this. You're at a business networking event, and you say hello to someone and ask, 'What do you do?' And they reply, 'I annoy burglars!'

Well, what are you going to say to that? Most likely, you're going to ask another question. Perhaps you'll ask, 'Tell me more?'

And the other person may reply, 'I'm a locksmith and security expert and my total focus for my clients is to ensure that they, their families and their business premises are totally safe and secure at all times. At no time has a property that I manage ever been burgled or security compromised.'

Wow, what will you say next? More importantly, will you remember this person at some future time if you are ever in the market for a security expert to assist you in your business or home? The chances are very high that you will, and if you had swapped business cards at the networking event, you may well call and ask for their assistance. You might even recommend them to people in your world if the chance arises, just because they stood out when you met them all that time ago.

That's the power of personal branding.

Think of those times you have recommended someone personally to a friend or colleague. You must really trust and rate them to do that; what is it about them that makes them stand out so much that you'd tell other people to give them a call? What is it about you that will make others do the same?

Everybody's heard of the word 'brand' and mostly we think about brands in relation to companies like McDonalds, Coke, Apple and Virgin. But think of those last two, Apple and Virgin, and the two people most associated with those companies; Steve Jobs and Sir Richard Branson. In his black jumper and steel-rimmed glasses, Steve Jobs never detracted from the Apple brand, he embodied it. The same is true of Richard Branson; he is a walking talking entrepreneur, he never wears a tie, is awkward in interviews, and his whole being is on the pulse of what his customers want, need and never even imagined possible.

Okay, you may be thinking, but these are two of the most successful people on the planet in recent history. How is personal branding really going to make a difference to my life or business?

How would you answer that question right now, 'What do you do?' Because the reality nowadays is that when people ask that question, what they really mean is 'Who are you?' And it's up to you whether your answer is a conversation starter or stopper. And what about your digital presence, what will people see if they Google your name before meeting you (and they always will)? Will they immediately get a clear sense of what you can offer them and how you'll do that?

When you pay attention to your personal brand, you begin to create a vision for your future, and with your personal brand strategy a path of action with which to get there. The impression you make, the interactions you have, the products you create and whether you are truly authentic and consistent are all key ingredients of personal branding and hugely impact your success as a business owner or employee throughout your career. It's time to stand up, stand out and be counted. What do you want people to think of when they hear your name? Who are the people you want to know your name? What can you offer them that will make their lives better, easier or happier?

Reputation has always been key to success and in today's digital and social media age you have more opportunities than ever before to build your reputation through your style, presence, connections, expertise, products and content. With just a little knowledge and dedicated time and effort, you can begin to influence all of those impressions and perceptions, and then build strong relationships that will in turn increase your value and open up your potential profits. As Kevin Roberts, former executive chairman of Saatchi & Saatchi, said to me in an interview, brands are no longer about business to business (b2b) or business to consumer (b2c) but are now all p2p, people to people.

**Don't leave your reputation to chance
when you can easily be your very own brand expert.**

Clarity, connection and communication are at the heart of your personal brand. When you have clarity around why it is that you do what you do for the customers or clients you serve, you embody a purpose that people can connect with; what you do is something that they want for themselves, whether it's the peace of mind offered by the security expert, the freedom offered by a time management consultant or the amazing body offered by a fitness coach. You walk the talk, everything you say and do builds recognition in your field, people begin to feel connected with you as you communicate across platforms and with increasing consistency. You're part of the conversation.

The best thing about personal branding is that our greatest success comes when we are truly being ourselves, rather than conforming. It's when we find our edge and no longer surrender to being generic that we stand out. The processes in this book allow us to explore what really makes us tick and what really makes us stand out. As soon as you are true to yourself, your personal brand begins to write itself.

When you have clarity around the key elements of your personal brand and you begin to create great content that you communicate consistently, it becomes so much easier to win clients and create powerful partnerships. You'll become more financially successful, too.

As you'll discover in the following chapters, there are a number of key tools with which you can define and then amplify your personal brand. You might narrow your niche in order to stand out in a less crowded marketplace. How do you use your website, social media platforms and professional sites to increase your online presence and connect with the people who matter to you? How do you build your network? And how can your personal brand help you to convert more leads into profits and success? How do you ensure there's consistency between your personal brand and your business model?

Right now you might be thinking, 'Oh, I don't want to be on social media, or online in any major way. I just want to quietly build my business and have the life I've envisioned for myself. Social media is for other people.' In the early days of the digital and social media evolution, you'd have been right in thinking that. But it's all changed. Everyone in business, whether you want to create a niche business and remain small or want to be the next Elon Musk, must stand out to get noticed. There's no ego attached to this anymore. It's just fundamental business marketing.

Follow the simple steps in this book and you will unlock the power and value of your personal brand to put you on the path to your own vision of personal success and a much more profitable business.

Chapter 1

What is Personal Branding in Business?

'Your brand is what other people say about you when you're not in the room.' - Jeff Bezos, CEO and Founder, Amazon

Imagine your colleagues or clients in a room together, at a drinks reception, and the main topic of conversation is you. How would they describe you to each other? Which of your characteristics would they identify? Which aspects of your personality, what you're really great at? Would they be able to describe what you do? Do you think they really value your strengths and skills? Perhaps you're not quite sure what they would say right now?

Simply put, branding has traditionally been the process involved in creating a unique name and image or perception for a product in the consumer's mind. The Mac 'Apple' immediately evokes a perception of style, creativity and efficiency. 'Kellogg's' says breakfast. 'Nike' says fashionable fitness. Brands promote an emotional response and when successful they increase customer loyalty, awareness and perceived value. As Kevin Roberts says, 'brand loyalty is where the money is, it's why your customers use you and choose you more often, you or your products are a part of their life, their own story. Apple isn't irreplaceable, but it is irresistible, so that we become loyal to the brand even beyond reason.'

Branding on a personal level does much the same thing. As Kevin says, it's all about people choosing you and then coming back and choosing you again, even telling everyone they know to come and choose you, too. Why should a potential client give up their hard earned cash to you, what are you offering them that will turn a 'maybe' into a 'yes'?

We might hope that it is the quality and content of our work that will naturally mean we stand out, but we also need the people who count (whether our team or our clients and customers) to perceive that quality for themselves and of course know that we even exist in the first place. These are the aspects of success that go beyond reason. You might be a wonderfully talented person inside, but unless you project your personality, expertise and general awesomeness to the world (or at least the people who matter in your world), you might lose out because people don't quite 'get' you and what you can do for them.

I know an acupuncturist in West London who is one of the most sought after fertility specialists in the whole of the UK. Just as Sir Richard Branson exudes entrepreneurial spirit with every breath, the moment people sit with Emma they feel her combination of warmth, experience, authority and engagement, and they just know that she cares and she is at the top of her field. Emma's personal brand has become her business brand; it's completely authentic and backed up by 20 years of experience. As a result, she can charge a premium for a premium value service, publishers want to publish her books, and all while doing work that she truly loves.

In another example, Sam owns a very successful carpet laying business in London. He has a strong work ethic and service culture within his business. As a result, he seldom loses a job that he's quoted for. His market niche is laying carpets and other flooring products in a small geographical area in London. He's captured that market and has substantially grown his team as a direct result of his success. He's built mutually beneficial relationships with an array of other trades and they refer work to each other very regularly. Sam's reputation is high with his referral partners and the community that he fully participates with in his personal life. That's the power of personal branding.

With the business world being even more competitive, the best and only way to stay ahead of the game is to make a connection with people and develop that love and loyalty through the unique combination of your expertise, experience, personality and passion, and your deep understanding of your community, your customers and your clients. Put these together and you'll soon get noticed for all the right reasons!

The 7+1 Pillars of Personal Brand Success

Have you ever wondered why in business some people stand taller and stronger, and have more impact, influence and success than others?

I guarantee you've noticed those people. They capture their market, time after time. They get media exposure. They have a successful business. They have a big community following them. And they have people wanting to associate and do business with them too. Whatever they touch seems to turn to gold.

Their profile and success makes you feel green with envy. And intuitively, you know their technical or business skills aren't any better than yours. These frustrations are realities in any business - traditional bricks and mortar businesses, and services businesses as well as online businesses. Some people seem to have the X factor and you can't put your finger on why. You ask, 'Why them and not me?'

The good news is that you can have that success, those wins, that profile and impact in your business too. It's available to all of us if we know what to do. Once upon a time (that's code for before the digital and social media age), it was much harder to have the public profile that many enjoy today. You had to pound the pavement, grease the right palms, have a convincing story and more... to get into the media, to get noticed.

That's all changed. It's now a level playing field and anyone can stand tall and stand out. It takes just seven steps. These are the seven key things that all 'those' people are doing:

1. They're clear about what they want to achieve.
2. They use their personality to endear themselves to others.
3. They have their 'patter' - their UVP or sales pitch - nailed.
4. They make a point of getting noticed where they want to be seen.
5. They offer products and services that people want.
6. They find people who want to do business with them, partnering with others.
7. They're profitable.

Oh, and there's one more thing. They work hard!

Simple! Or is it? I can hear you say, 'well I do all that too!' We all do some of that. But do you have a full-on strategy or a system around all that? Is there a key element missing that could be the tipping point for your personal brand and success? The real winners – those who really get noticed and achieve the success that many of us aspire to – have total clarity and commitment to what they're doing and why they are doing it.

They embrace what I call the **7+1 Pillars of Personal Branding** that support them to stand tall, stand out, and get noticed:

Passion – they live and breathe what they do in business and life. We can feel their passion. They are dreamers who are full of vision. They're on a journey, a mission, they live and work with purpose, and we want to go with them.

Personalisation – gone are the days where we show everyone just the bits of us we want people to see. Now it's about seeing the real person. That's how communities are created, it determines whether people pay attention and why followers follow. We get to know them – warts and all! It's become personal.

Positioning – they know what their market is; they are niched and proud of that niche. They aren't trying to be everything to everybody. They love the people who make up their market - their community – and they know how to position themselves as experts or authorities in that market so people connect with them and their message.

Platforms – this is the really exciting part. Regular people are achieving extraordinary success and getting noticed by putting their message out to their market by choosing the platforms that work for them. It might be a combination of networking, blogging, any or all of the social media channels, writing books, guest speaking, hosting webinars, creating YouTube videos, running a podcast... the possibilities are endless. They are available for everyone, and branded people are using them.

Products – they serve the market they're focused on with products that are relevant. The products and services they offer vary – free offers, lower entry offers, midpriced products, high priced/premium products. We can all do this, regardless of our business - it's 'out of the box thinking' - seeing things differently.

Partnerships – people want to partner and be associated with branded people as the relationship is mutually beneficial. It's not a one way road. Branded people are connected to other 'movers and shakers' in their world, and they work together.

Profitability – to be truly successful, we must ensure our business model is profitable, so that our business interests reflect positively on our personal brand.

They are the 7 **Pillars of Personal Branding.**

And what's the +1?

Performance – personal branding success comes with commitment, discipline, resilience, time and hard work. Full stop!

The 7+1 pillars to standing tall in business are there for the taking, for you and everyone you compete with in your market. Are you going to take the plunge and become your very own brand?

ACTION

Learn from others in your industry or those whom you admire. Ask yourself:

Who are the leaders in my niche?

_____

_____

_____

_____

What stands them apart from me?

_____

_____

_____

_____

What is their offering?

_____

_____

_____

_____

How do they get noticed?

_____

_____

_____

_____

_____

What platforms are they using?

_____

_____

_____

_____

_____

What is the business model they apply in their business?

_____

_____

_____

_____

_____

What partnerships do they have?

_____

_____

_____

_____

_____

Chapter 2

Why Brand Yourself?

> 'When you brand yourself properly, the competition becomes irrelevant.' – Anon

What do you want to be known for in business? What impact do you want to make on the world? Is this immediately apparent to others either when they meet you in person or, more likely, when they look you up before meeting you? Don't underestimate who you are and what you know, and when it comes to your personal brand what you are capable of being for someone else.

Over one billion names are searched on Google every single day, and the information they find for you will go some way towards affecting whether they decide to do business with you or simply get in touch with you. It will affect their perceived value of you and what you do, and frequently our first impressions are formed at this virtual stage before we even meet people. So it's crucial to cover all aspects of our personal branding and make sure they are aligned, both online and in person. When your personal brand aligns with your values and what you are passionate about, which might simply be the kinds of tasks you love doing, you get to do what you are meant to do and be successful at it.

Let's take a look at seven great reasons for creating and maintaining your personal brand in business.

1. Establish Your Credibility

When you take the time to really get to the heart of who you are and what you do, you begin to build a personal brand that others will trust because what you are promising is what you deliver. When you provide value to others on a steady basis, you soon begin to establish your credibility and build that trust factor, which is one of your greatest promotional assets. Word of mouth travels fast, and won't even cost you a penny. You are creating a movement from the ground up when you understand exactly what it is you have to offer, it's much easier for people to bond with you when you know what you stand for.

2. Differentiate Yourself

We live in an intensively competitive world and it's only through personal branding that you can really identify what makes you different and use that to stand out amongst the crowd. Each one of us is a unique combination of skills, experiences, values and passions, so that we each have something unique to offer. Perhaps you have the advantage of a personal story that will really connect with your customers/audience, or you have identified a key problem you can offer a solution for that no one else in your field has addressed. Perhaps you stand out because of your style. Whatever makes you different, in a good way, will help you build both your brand and your success.

3. Focus on the Work that Matters

As you go through the personal branding process, your self-awareness will increase, deepening your understanding of yourself and what makes you unique, powerful and valuable. This in turn will lead you to focusing more on work that utilises your unique qualities (and is therefore of more value to others) rather than trying to be all things to all people.

4. Increase Your Visibility

When you narrow your focus on your strengths and identify your target audience you will become much more visible to the people who really matter; your potential customers/clients/employers, and also the people in your field who are considered to be the influencers, who will help to bring you more customers. Because you've taken care to really think about your personal brand and what it is that you can offer, you will appear as someone trustworthy and a go-to expert.

5. Build Your Network

A brand is nothing without engagement. Growing your network is crucial for business success; it opens doors to opportunities you would have never thought of. Your personal brand is similar to a magnet; it attracts likeminded people who can be very useful to you and your business. When you have clarity around your purpose, values, and your offer, the power of attraction will grow stronger.

6. Magnetise Opportunities

As a result of your growing network, not only are people more willing to help you, but they will actually provide you with more opportunities, which could be a new business idea, a joint venture, co-writing books or a customer referral. When you have a strong, authentic and memorable brand that consistently delivers, people will always be willing to recommend you to others and want to work with you in the future. You will be able to monetise many of these opportunities so your business will become more profitable.

7. Build Your Value

As you build your personal brand with passion, personality and outstanding performance, your value will grow, both in your own mind and for your customers or clients.

ACTION

Be honest. Ask yourself:

What are the benefits of me being branded?

_____
_____
_____
_____
_____
_____

How will I differentiate myself from my competitors?

_____
_____
_____
_____
_____
_____

What excites me most about having a visible personal brand?

_____
_____
_____
_____
_____
_____

PART TWO: Build Your Personal Brand

The Personal Brand Star System™ is my own framework for guiding business owners and entrepreneurs around the world who are creating their own personal brand. Why a star? Think of the Hollywood Walk of Fame where certain streets are paved with the stars of famous people; people who are recognised as being at the top of their game.

I want the same for you. I want you to build your personal brand so you're recognised as the leader or expert in your business niche. I want you to stand head and shoulders above your competition so that when potential customers in your niche are seeking someone who provides the products and services you offer, your name is on the top of their list of suppliers. I want you to be the star of your business niche. I want you to enjoy profitable business success, as you define it, through the power of your personal brand.

Here's a visual image of what my Personal Brand Star System™ looks like.

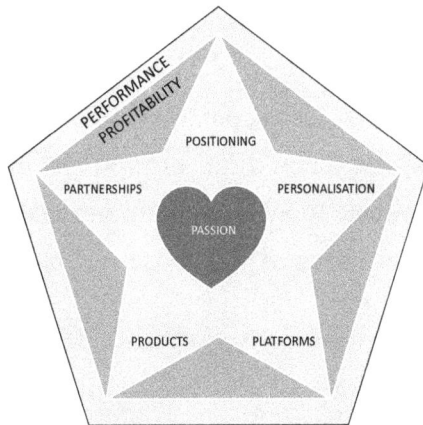

In this section of the book we are going to explore each of the 7+1 Pillars of my Personal Brand Star System™ so that you have all the tools you need to articulate and amplify your personal brand in your own niche.

It all starts with passion, because when there is true passion at the heart of your personal brand, everything else works together more seamlessly. When you put your passions at the centre then you are being true to yourself, which makes it so much easier to position yourself to the right people who need exactly what it is you have to offer and who like the way you work. You become the 'go-to' person for a community or a demographic because your pitch and your presentation are music to their ears. You have the confidence to be yourself so that people are able to connect with your personal brand even more strongly. Your style is your personal brand, the way you talk and the stories you tell, these all add personalisation - the colour and detail that will mean people remember you for all the right reasons.

Once you are clear about your passions, your positioning and how you can personalise your brand, you will then be able to focus more effectively on using the right platforms to amplify your personal brand, in other words, let people know about your existence, your expertise and why they should come to you for what you offer. These platforms are available to all of us both online and offline and with so many available we need to pick those which will be most valuable and bring the best ROI.

When I talk about 'products' in relation to your personal brand, I mean anything that has 'you' in it, from a blog or video to ebooks and tip series. When your business is you, developing the right products is clearly essential for profits and success, but even if your business is selling equipment, plumbing or hairdressing, you can create products that utilise your personal brand for the benefit of the business. Teaching people how to use equipment, maintenance tips, or an evening introduction to hair and colour - these are all products that raise your personal brand and your business to another level.

When we know who we are, what we are offering and where we want to be, it is then possible to form partnerships that are beneficial to all, especially our customers and clients. Because you have spent time on developing your personal brand, you will know when potential partnerships feel aligned, you can come together with others to combine your strengths, share resources and reach new audiences.

All these pillars of personal branding are crucial, but that dedicated time and effort can go to waste unless we figure out how to turn our new and improved personal brand into profits. The good news is you will have laid all the foundations you need, so with my blueprint you will soon be turning your personal brand into profitability and success.

It all takes one thing, which I call performance. We have to be willing to put in the work required, and as soon as we are, the positive results can seriously start flowing in. You need to have a strategy, which you will develop as you go through the next seven chapters, and then a focused and achievable plan of action, which I will show you how to put together.

So let's get started and really hone in on what makes you tick, how your passions form the foundation of why you do what you do for the people you do it for.

Chapter 3

Passion

'Knowing yourself is the beginning of all wisdom.' - Aristotle

Are you beginning to see the power of personal branding and the impact it might have on your own business? What would really help to grow your business right now? Is it the trust factor that will get more people saying yes to your offer? Or the partnerships that will flow through networking and recommendation? Are you in a competitive market right now so you can see the benefit of pinpointing what really makes you stand out? Or can you see how understanding your strengths more clearly will help you to choose the opportunities that will bring you the greatest success and fulfilment?

You might feel like you aren't in a position right now to spend time or resources on something that you aren't actually paid for. Shouldn't you just get on with paying the bills and bringing in the business? But, if you were to never spend any time identifying what makes you stand out, then how will you stand out? If you didn't put together a strategy and plan for how you're going to communicate your expertise to more of the people who matter, more often, then you'd be doing yourself and what you do a disservice. And as a result you may find it hard to imagine how you would ever be able to put a premium value on what you do – how you will be able to grow. If you don't value yourself, how will anyone else?

The good news is that you already have a valuable brand, you just need the clarity to see it and then communicate it; for example, through your personal website, appearance, LinkedIn profile, social media activity and networking. Because once you start doing that on a regular basis, your personal brand will become one of your greatest business assets for growth, development and success.

Understanding Yourself - Your Purpose, Vision and Values

To start the personal branding process and get off on the right foot we need to find out what is at the heart of you. This chapter is about understanding you. We will focus on key areas of finding and defining who you are as a person; your passions, values, strengths, personal attributes, experience, vision and goals. If you don't spend time understanding yourself, then it will be difficult for others to get to know the real you who is unique. You might be making all the right noises and meeting all the right people but unless you are fully present as yourself, others may find it hard to really connect with you, especially in the long term.

As you get to know yourself, you can then assess how other people perceive you, and how you wish to be perceived. Where do you belong, and are you pitching to the right people?

From answering these key questions you will find the elements that combine to create your unique personal brand that reveal what makes you and what you do something that is really worth talking about. And the clearer you become, the more others will talk about you and your brand too, so that you become a magnet for the right kind of people and opportunities suited to you and you begin to focus on the work that matters both to your success and happiness.

Brand YOU – Uncovering the Heart of Your Passion

Understanding the concept of branding yourself has to do with first uncovering who you are as a person. Your brand isn't an ad campaign or a tagline; it's a combination of your beliefs, interests, talents, strengths, experiences and values. Personal branding is not an act or a display for others. It's you being you and nothing more. But sometimes it isn't immediately easy to know or say what being 'me' is. We can look at our friends or colleagues and see their strengths shining through, but we feel less certain about our own. It's time to unlock the dam of uncertainty and let your dreams, thoughts and the real you flow.

So, what are the characteristics and qualities that combine to make you 'you'? Take a break from your schedule to ask yourself, 'Who am I and what defines me?' Spending time answering these questions is the start of the journey towards guiding you to do the work that inspires and motivates you.

Here are four questions that will help to uncover these characteristics:

1. What are my experiences?
2. What are my strengths?

3. What am I passionate about?

4. What are my values?

Don't over think this exercise. Grab a big piece of paper and put down the first things that come into your mind. If you need help getting started, brainstorm with someone you trust who won't put words in your mouth but will allow and encourage you to explore. You might ask your partner, family, friends, relatives, co-workers what words come to mind when they think of you. I'm quite sure everybody will have something to say about you, and no matter what it is, take notes. These will all be helpful insights into how people perceive you. Be aware that they may or may not match up with how you want to be perceived. But if you ask those close to you, or people you know to be perceptive, chances are they will have a good idea of the real you that shines from within.

This is not an idle exercise. This is the start of working out what defines you. This will lead you to what I call your 'heart of passion'. It might sound soft and fluffy, but unless people feel, sense and hear your passion, they won't be drawn to you.

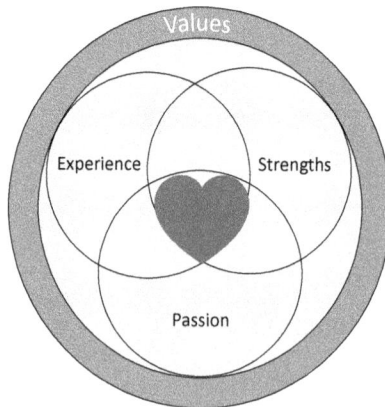

As an image, the heart of passion looks like this.

When we bring your experience, strengths and passions together with your values wrapped around them, the intersection is your 'sweet spot'. The sweet spot or heart is where the gold dust lies. When we extract this from your mind and analyse it, we can then start to see what you should be doing and how to position you and your personal brand to ensure you stand out from the crowd in your market in that niche.

Let's take a closer look at the elements of your heart of passion.

Experience

We accumulate experience via our qualifications, work history and life's journey. Don't be shy, write all your experiences down.

Strengths

We have all have skills and strengths. Strengths are those abilities we have that are more than just a skill. They are absolute attributes, often we use them daily. We excel at them and we rely on them in business and in life. We get energy from them.

For instance, my skills include: leadership, people management, understanding numbers (I'm a Chartered Accountant by qualification), business strategy, time management, and many others.

Yet the key strengths I rely on day by day and that are reported on in all assessments I've undertaken over the years include: being a visionary, leadership, communication and presentation skills, relationship building, results orientation, infectious enthusiasm, problem solving, learning and teaching.

There are some excellent tools available to help you identify your core strengths. In understanding those, you'll be guided into doing work that fully utilises those strengths and leading you away from working in areas that accentuate your weaknesses or use skills you have that don't energise you. The worst task or activity for me in my businesses would be doing book keeping and monthly accounting work. Even though I can do it, and it's a skill I have, it's not an area of strength. I am not energised by this task. Therefore, that work gets delegated.

If you want to do more work on understanding your strengths, I recommend the following online assessments:

- Gallup Strengths Finder 2.0 (sometimes known as the Clifton Strengths Finder 2.0)
- Insights Discovery Profile

Passion

What are you passionate about? What inspires and motivates you? Don't be limited here. Think freely — think about all your passions in business and life.

The heart of passion

The heart of passion is the intersection of the three circles. Once the work is done in the three circles, hopefully you can distil it all into your sweet spot, and create or evolve your business within the sweet spot, and develop your personal brand around it.

Let's look at an example. Meet James. He has an excellent fulltime job in a senior accounting role, and he's building a second business as an Accounting Exam Coach, inspiring and guiding accounting students to prepare for exams. While in the early stages of development, you can tell from his experience, strengths, passions and values that he's well suited to this work. He's currently creating frameworks that will support him to scale and monetise the business. James is exploring the viability of this business being his full-time work in the future. Here's a summary of James's heart of passion.

Experience	Strengths	Passions	Values
Accounting qualifications Experience as an accountant and auditor working in public practice and a financial controller in industry Lecturing in accounting	Learning and teaching Tenacity - ability to overcome his own challenges in life Inspiring others to master mindset and to achieve	Helping accounting students pass professional exams through learning how to work, study and mentally prepare	Accountability Achievement Courage Hard Work Learning Leadership Optimism Self-reliance

Strengths aligned with passions

At school, we're often conditioned to focus on improving our weaknesses rather than building on our strengths. I'm all for receiving a well-rounded education, but when it comes to business it's all too easy to fall into the trap of spending all our energy on trying to fix what we're not so good at instead of changing our business model to work with what we're awesome at and that excites and energises us!

Again, see which strengths you recognise above all others. How are you putting them to use in your business and life right now, and could you develop more ways to make the most use of them? Are you a problem solver through your ingenuity or your conscientiousness and caring? Do you gain the most pleasure from helping others? Or are you an amazing team player who will always keep everyone going to the finish line?

I was running a day long workshop for creative entrepreneurs who were all at similar stages in their businesses; and for whom developing their sense of personal branding was a crucial key to unlocking each of their potentials. After about an hour, they spontaneously invited each other to describe how they saw the others in the group. One woman had described herself as a 'writer', but another perceived her in much greater, more vivid detail, 'you listen intently, zoning in on the words, analysing their relevance and feeling their vibration'. Which description stands out more for you?

Passion Doesn't Equal Purpose

Many think that when they have found their passion, therein lies their purpose – that 'thing' they should be doing in life and often in business. That isn't so. Passion is only one part of the purpose equation.

Purpose – what is it?

Finding your purpose in business means being able to answer the questions: 'What do I do for my customers, and why do I do it? And in being successful in achieving my purpose for my customers, what's my 'why' for me, my family and lifestyle?'

Purpose is a simple equation.

What + Why = Purpose

What are you doing?

You answered that in the heart of passion work you did. You've worked out what you are or should be doing, now you can focus on the 'why'.

Why?

In order to answer the 'why' questions, you must check two things.

In doing the work you want to do, is there a need for it? What problem are you solving by doing what you do? What's the gap in the market you can fill?

If you can answer that, then you must check that the need is financially viable, otherwise you're not creating a viable business.

You've got a hobby instead.

Let's analyse it some more.

Your customer 'why': Are you solving a problem that exists and can you make money in solving that problem?

Your personal 'why': In being successful in your business for your customers, does this business and your purpose serve you personally? Will it pay you the income you want to give you the lifestyle you desire?

Your purpose described

If you can answer 'yes' to all the 'why' questions, then there is a marriage with your 'why' and 'what'. You have your purpose. You can now go for it in business... and brand yourself as the 'go-to' person, the expert in that niche. You can create your purpose statement so that when you're asked the question: 'What do you do?', you'll be clear and focused in your response.

For example, the purpose for my brand *Small Business Huge Success*™ is 'to inform, inspire and impact small business owners and entrepreneurs around the world to achieve profitable growth and extraordinary success by collaborating with other business experts, and creating, curating and hosting summits, workshops, conferences, and publishing books on topics related to small business growth and success'.

Values

You must infuse the 'Brand You' with your values. Your personal values will serve you professionally – they surround your heart of passion.

You may be asking, 'What are values?'

Values are those things or ideals that we believe are important to us. They're the principles or standards of behaviour, or our internal rules. Values govern the way we operate and behave. What do you expect from yourself and others? What qualities do you aim to bring to your interactions with people? What are your guiding principles?

Michael Henderson and Dougal Thompson in their excellent book, *Values at Work*, describe values as 'the sum of our preferences and priorities. Preferences are what we would rather have in our lives than do without. Priorities indicate how important each preference is in relation to another. A value can therefore be described as a preference, multiplied by its priority.'

Values are descriptors of what is important to us – in business and life. While abstract in nature as words, they have meaning when they are brought to life, when they are experienced and lived.

Why are values important in business and personally?

People and organisations that have strong values are more focused. When values are clear, they provide direction and draw attention to what is important. When shared across a business, if the leaders fully engage staff in the importance of the values to the business, then there is an expectation that all staff will live and breathe the values too. If not, then there is a potential for cultural mismatch. People will only support a business's values if they match their own. Role performance will be heightened when there is values alignment between the people and the business. Sir Richard Branson's Virgin Group is a values based business, and Branson's personal values and those of Virgin are in complete alignment. He lives and breathes his values in life and in business. Zappos, the hugely successful American online shoe retailer led by Tony Hsieh, is renowned for its strong values and corporate culture. If people join the company and find there is a cultural mismatch, the company encourages them to leave immediately, and they give them a severance payment to do so, as the company recognises the effect of 'one bad apple' on the rest.

Values are as important to small businesses as they are to large ones. If you are a one person business or solopreneur, your personal values will likely be your business values. They will support you in life and in your business. If you live and breathe your values, others will likely sense what your values are by your actions and behaviours (both good and bad). People will warm to you if you're living your values, if they resonate with them. As your business grows, if you recruit for values, you're more likely to have cultural alignment between you, your company and your team.

Identifying your values

Below I've included a list of values to help begin this process. Sit quietly for a few minutes and consider the words and how you resonate with them. Which do you genuinely feel really comfortable and positive with? Don't go for words that you believe should be your values. We all grow up surrounded with other people's values and what we perceive we should be if we are going to be successful. Use your own experiences as a guide. As you notice how the words resonate with you, think of the times in your life when you felt happiest and most fulfilled. Which values were you engaging in during those times?

Circle up to 10 values.

Accountability	Curiosity	Freedom	Mastery	Shrewdness
Accuracy	Decisiveness	Friends	Merit	Simplicity
Achievement	Democraticness	Fun	Obedience	Soundness
Adventurousness	Dependability	Generosity	Openness	Speed
Altruism	Determination	Goodness	Optimism	Spirituality
Ambition	Devoutness	Grace	Order	Spontaneity
Assertiveness	Diligence	Gratitude	Originality	Stability
Balance	Discipline	Growth	Partnership	Strategic
Being the best	Discretion	Happiness	Patriotism	Strength
Belonging	Diversity	Hard work	Perfection	Structure
Boldness	Dynamism	Health	Piety	Success
Calmness	Economy	Helping Society	Positivity	Support
Carefulness	Effectiveness	Holiness	Practicality	Teaching
Challenge	Efficiency	Honesty	Preparedness	Teamwork
Cheerfulness	Elegance	Honour	Professionalism	Temperance
Choice	Empathy	Humility	Prudence	Thankfulness
Clear-mindedness	Enjoyment	Independence	Quality-orientation	Thoroughness
Collaboration	Enthusiasm	Ingenuity	Relationships	Thoughtfulness
Commitment	Entrepreneurship	Inner Harmony	Reliability	Timeliness
Community	Equality	Inquisitiveness	Resourcefulness	Tolerance
Compassion	Excellence	Insightfulness	Restraint	Traditionalism
Competitiveness	Excitement	Intelligence	Results-oriented	Travel
Consistency	Experiences	Intellectual Status	Rigor	Trustworthiness
Contentment	Expertise	Intuition	Security	Truth-seeking
Continuous improvement	Exploration	Investment	Self-actualization	Understanding
Contribution	Expressiveness	Joy	Self-control	Uniqueness
Control	Fairness	Justice	Self Development	Unity
Conversation	Faith	Leadership	Self Improvement	Usefulness
Cooperation	Family-orientedness	Learning	Selflessness	Vision
Correctness	Fidelity	Legacy	Self-reliance	Vitality
Courage	Fitness	Love	Sensitivity	Wealth
Courtesy	Fluency	Loyalty	Serenity	Wellbeing
Creativity	Focus	Making a difference	Service	Wonder

Now you can look for the themes and begin to prioritise your values. For example, if you had circled 'contribution' and 'generosity' or 'continuous improvement' and 'growth' you can begin to ask yourself which of those is more important if you had to choose between them.

Identifying your values gives you the gift of clarity, both as you develop your personal brand and as you travel through your professional and personal life. When you have that niggling feeling about a difficult choice you need to make; for example, whether to work with a particular person or create a particular product, you can access your values and use them as guides. What do they tell you? To go for it and enjoy the ride or look for a route that will in the long run serve you and others better? Often, we think we are meant to make important decisions with our head, when the guide we might be better off listening to is our heart.

This is how you get to do the work you love and love the work you do. It's how you create a business that attracts customers and employees with complementary values. It means you'll be able to speak to them with your own authentic voice, which in turns leads to trust and loyalty. The specific words you use to describe your values won't be set in stone as life is a journey and how we see ourselves will always be subject to change and growth, for example your definition of 'success' may change over time and with experience, but the underlying principles are an intrinsic part of what makes you 'you'.

Vision

You've probably heard the word 'vision' bandied about in business. A vision is a descriptive aspiration of what you want your business to achieve. It's the descriptor of your dream. For me DREAM means: Destiny, Represented Evocatively, Actively and Magnetically.

What is your DREAM for your business? How will building your personal brand support you in achieving that dream?

Imagine the future; you're looking back on your life and saying to yourself, 'I did it. I did it!'

What does that 'it' look like for you? What is your potential realised? Take a few minutes now with a blank piece of paper and don't just imagine it, but bring it to life.

When you do this exercise, I encourage you to manifest mindfulness; turn up your inner voice and allow yourself to write freely about all your dreams. Some may be professional, while others may be personal. How does your life look when they come together in harmony? What are you doing? Where are you? What have you created? Do you have a legacy or have you tread lightly, helping people along the way?

You may prefer to write your vision, or use an image vision board with pictures you can find online or in magazines, your own drawings, use anything you like! When you bring your vision out of your head and begin to describe it and give it substance, you take the first steps towards making it happen.

Your vision is at the heart of your personal brand. It's the best version of you and your life that you can think of; it's you living and working with purpose and realising your potential. When you have clarity over your vision, your purpose will deliver it for you via your business strategy which we talk more about in chapter 9.

Go For the Opportunities You Really Want

It's not only other people who get to see your unique combination of personality, strengths and passions when you develop your personal brand; you will also have a clearer picture of what it is that you want out of life and what you want to achieve. There are a lot of 'shoulds' and 'oughts' in life and even more choices. If we only ever did what other people expected or wanted from us, would we ever really be our true selves, performing at our best?

If your heart isn't in it, whatever it is, there is a way forward, and getting to know yourself and what you stand for deep down is the first step towards making a change. It might be a case of rediscovering the things about your business that you love, but that have become subsumed by other tasks that drain your motivation. Or perhaps it really is time to delegate work, so you focus on those activities and tasks that energise you and use your strengths.

The more confident you feel in your personal brand, the easier it will be to take your next step. If you just had a sense that things weren't quite right but you haven't figured out what you stand for and what you love, then it's going to be extremely difficult to spot the opportunities that are likely to be right for you, let alone know how to go for them and grab them. Likewise, let's say you have a small start-up business. You might feel like you're constantly chasing around, working on projects that aren't quite building up into anything substantial. You're busy, no question, but it feels as though you're being pulled in various directions and getting nowhere rather than forging ahead.

This is where your personal brand starts to be of incredible value to your business and even your happiness. When you know what your values are, you are able to sense which people you know you're going to enjoy working with and those with whom there might be a conflict of purpose or personality. When you know what your passions are and where your strengths lie, you realise it doesn't do anyone any favours when you try and force yourself to do a project or a deal that isn't aligned with who you are. You won't shine in those situations, and so if they are vitally necessary as a stepping stone along the way, always try to find elements that light your passion in some way.

Summary

In this chapter we have done a lot of work to uncover your passions so that when you come to write that LinkedIn profile or pitch for that project you know you are perfect for, you will present yourself and your personal brand in alignment. Your core values create the foundation of your personal brand, they add strength and depth to whatever is presented on the surface level. This is the key to instilling your brand with integrity and growing the potential value of what you do. Once you have an understanding of who you are and what makes you tick, it makes it so much easier to position yourself and find the right customers and clients for you.

ACTION

What does your heart of passion look like?

_____

_____

_____

_____

_____

Why do you do what you do for your customers?

_____

_____

_____

_____

_____

Why do you do what you do for you and your family?

_____

_____

_____

_____

_____

Is there a need in the market for your work?

_____

_____

_____

_____

Can you monetise that opportunity in the market?

_____

_____

_____

_____

If you can monetise that opportunity in the market, is it sufficient to build a business and pay you a good salary?

_____

_____

_____

_____

_____

If you can monetise that opportunity in the market, what is the vision you've created for your business?

_____

_____

_____

_____

Elon Musk

**'If something is important enough, you should try,
even if the probable outcome is failure.'**

Elon Musk is the South-African born entrepreneur, inventor and engineer behind some of the most forward thinking brands and companies in the world: Tesla, SpaceX and SolarCity. His style has a swagger to it but as a force of nature who also sees the power of nature he has become the renegade hero of renewable energy, showing that eco warriors can be stylish too; you'll never see him without a jacket.

Musk is a man on a quest, and that energy and attitude makes him instantly recognisable. He's a modern day pioneer and explorer; his grand vision is to colonise Mars, believing it to be the only way to save our civilisation. So, whether you think he's arrogant or egotistical to even consider such grandiose ideas, you don't forget Elon Musk in a hurry.

He has been a voracious entrepreneur from a young age, making a reported $22 million from his first start-up and approximately $250 million for his part in the creation of PayPal and subsequent sale to Ebay.

His latest endeavour at the time of this book going to print (because with Elon Musk you never quite know what is going to come next) is the announcement of OpenAI, a billion dollar not for profit company founded with Sam Altman, president of the startup incubator Y Combinator. They wish to develop the technology for artificial intelligence and make that technology freely available to all so that there won't be one company that holds all the cards and therefore the power. Musk and Altman also just happen to now have access to some of the top minds in the engineering and data industries, making it likely that some very interesting innovations will come out of the project in the shorter term while AI is likely to take many decades.

Musk's personal brand reflects the dynamism and tenacity of the man. When you build a car that scores 103 points out of 100 in the Consumer Reports rating, it suggests you might not be the meek and mild type. Musk has said in interviews how concerned he is about the possibility of an AI apocalypse, and yet not only does he then found a company to develop AI technology but he is already forging ahead with developing self-driving Tesla cars.

And it certainly doesn't mean everyone likes him; according to one biography he had harsh words for a male employee who missed a Tesla event for the birth of his child. He has been married three times and has employed a nanny manager for his five children's nannies. But he has also moved green energy forward more rapidly than anyone could have imagined and the fact that we know about the quirks and difficult bits of Musk's character adds an authenticity and therefore strength to his brand. What you see is what you get. Musk himself says little about his personal life and focuses on his projects and his passions. He is incredibly hard working, unafraid of failure and doesn't give up. He never stops learning and everything he does stems from his inner passion, reflects his personality, engages his skills and indulges his inner space geek.

Chapter 4

Positioning

> 'Too many people overvalue what they are not and undervalue what they are.' - Malcolm Forbes, Publisher

Once you understand who you are, what you do, and why you do it, you can identify your audience, the people who will benefit most from what you have to offer. Personal branding isn't a one way street; the most successful brands and people not only know themselves but also their customers or clients, readers or patients, and then match up the style, tone and offer of one with the style, tone and needs of the other. In other words, your personal brand needs precision positioning if you are going to maximise your potential, and increase the profitability and success of your business.

Think back to the locksmith at the networking event. When asked what he does, he replies with his purpose; he is a 'security expert' whose number one focus is to keep his customers 100 percent safe and secure at all times. We have the impression he is knowledgeable about the best security products available, we can trust his expertise and he appears to really care, which suggests he will be reliable and as good as his word. He has also identified the people most likely to value his services – those with families or business premises they wish to protect.

Meet Dr Lucille Henry, a friend and business collaborator of mine. Dr Henry guides her clients – business owners/entrepreneurs and executives – through the emotional obstacles that block their path forward, teaching them how to connect to a stronger sense of self so they achieve the outcomes and success they desire. With a background in scientific research, gaining a PhD in biochemistry and working as a research fellow for 10 years, Dr Henry brings a very practical and common sense approach to healing techniques and a clear and different positioning to others who are in this field of work – not many healers start their careers as research scientists. She's also an author. Dr Henry's market positioning or unique value proposition (UVP) is crystal clear so that she can effectively market directly to her target audience.

Your Personal Brand Value Statement

Now that you have identified your purpose and values, and have begun to put together a vision of where you want to be in business and life, you can harness that knowledge and energy to create your personal brand value proposition or your UVP. Your UVP not only conveys who you are and what you do but it positions you in terms of your target audience and places a value on what you offer or do, for example by identifying a need and providing a solution, or how you help or enhance people's lives.

To create your UVP, you need to explore and answer three questions:

1. Who are you serving and what are their problems and ambitions? (your target audience)

2. What are you best at, how can you help with those problems and ambitions? (your value)

3. How are you different from others in your niche? (your UVP)

Who Are You Serving?

Once you've dug deep inside the cosmic sandbox of 'yourself', and found the substance that makes you unique, you have uncovered your essence, the foundation of your personal brand, and it leads naturally to the next step of finding your people, your audience, your potential customers.

Just as we can't all be experts at everything, we can't be all things to all people. The reason why personal branding has become such an important element in business success is in this simple idea that nobody wants to buy something from a person who can do everything for everyone. Figure out the target audience that would actually benefit from you and your service/expertise and zero in on connecting with and developing a relationship with them.

Are you talking to the right people? Do you know who the right people are? What specific need are you addressing for those people? When I ask my clients to describe their ideal customer or client avatar, it's often one of the hardest things for them to do, especially when I ask them to get really specific. The more targeted your niche, the clearer and stronger your personal brand will be within that group.

For instance, are you a tech geek, social dynamite, fashionista or foodie? If you are a 'foodie', what's your niche within that huge area: is it healthy food, vegan food, baking or fine dining? Say you are a 'coach'; expand on that, are you a career coach, a fitness coach, a finance coach? A popular term that people use now, coined by Seth Godin, is to think of your 'tribe'. Again, when you describe your group or tribe, it should feel like a good fit with your values, strengths and passions. Do you feel like you have something really great to contribute to this group, to teach them, entertain them, solve problems for them, give them a fantastic service or inspire them? Yes? Then you're on the path to finding your people.

If you want to succeed in the business world with your personal brand, then you need to have a crystal clear picture of who your ideal audience is, and how you're going to engage them. You can even create your very own vision board filled with rich information that you've gathered. Unless you have clarity over who your ideal customer is your marketing will end up being generic and often ineffective.

So, the best way to find out your target audience is to write out a description of who you're looking to attract. What they look like, what they do, how they act, demographics, their needs, wants and problems, location, your feelings towards them and their feelings towards you. You must tap into what their challenges are; you must connect with them at a deeply emotional level. If you do that, there is a much greater chance they'll believe you understand their problems, challenges, goals and aspirations, and they'll more likely want to connect with you.

The best customer avatar you can create is one where you're talking to a specific person – a composite character who represents real people, where you fully understand their needs, wants and problems.

Here are some questions you must ask yourself as you begin to identify your target market:

- What are their demographics: sex, age, marital status?
- What is their location?
- What do they like to do for social activities?
- What do they like to do for cultural sustenance?
- What are their personal values?
- What is their vision in business and/or life?
- What is their work/job/experience or expertise?
- What are the problems you solve for them?

Hopefully you're getting the idea. The more deeply you delve into the demographics and psychographics of your perfect customer, the more you understand and can market to and serve them. This list of questions is not exhaustive. If you're serious about identifying your customer avatar, then please download my free customer avatar questionnaire and a sample of a customer avatar at: www.smallbusinesshugesuccess.com/personalbranding

You may be thinking, 'What's so important about creating a customer avatar when talking about personal branding?' By targeting your marketing to your customers, when they feel you understand them and their world – their problems, challenges, goals and aspirations – they will begin to emotionally connect with you. They'll see you as the go-to person to work with. Trust starts being built. If you're constantly 'on message' in all the marketing you do, whether it be in your blogs, videos, social media activity or presentations, you'll continue to demonstrate empathy, so the trust deepens. This goes a long way towards creating a long term and sustainable business, because when your potential customers need or want what it is you sell, hopefully they'll turn to you to buy from.

Finding Your Value

One of the biggest challenges is to place the right value on what you do and therefore begin to take steps towards the levels of success and profit that match your potential. There's nothing more frustrating than running around working all hours of the day and at the end of the day feeling undervalued. If you feel that way, the first person who needs to know more clearly what value you can offer is you.

When you define the value you provide to others, then you start to answer their WIIFM question, 'what's in it for me?'. Your target audience, whether clients, customers, colleagues or employers, needs to know exactly who you are and how you're going to be the solution to their problems. You need to do the valuable work. They want to know two simple things:

1. They need to be sure you care for them.
2. They need to know exactly how you are going to help them.

Value List

Write down 30 ways you can help your target audience. These will show you all the ways you can go the extra mile and stand out. Make sure that these are all promises that you can keep, so be realistic as well as creative in your thinking.

Problem / need / desire	Solution you can provide

Customer Promise

So, you've now identified all the ways in which you add value for the customer. The big question now is what stands you apart from your competitors? Why are you different? Why should a potential customer select you over your competitor? Please don't say that 'you offer good service or better service'. That's not enough, and besides, the idea of service is so subjective. One person may think you give exceptional service, while another may think you're just pretty average.

What truly stands you apart? It's not that you have to do one thing ten times better. Perhaps you do ten things one percent better. How do you go the extra mile?

Are you faster, more convenient or more flexible than your competition?

Is it your style that sets you apart? Are you generic or a one off? Like Marmite not everyone is going to like working with you or using your service, but enough people will LOVE it.

Do you talk to your customers about what is truly important to them? Do you really listen to their problems so that you can offer the best solution? Do you show enough that you care?

Do you take the time to de-mystify processes or products for people?

What emotions do you want people to take away after working with/buying from you? Can these form a part of your promise?

Can you become even more specialist? Your promise will be even clearer if you can.

It's important to get past any self doubts or anxiety about people thinking you're not as good as you say you are. Know what your promise is and make it to the people who matter.

Keywords for Personal Brand Positioning

Being personally branded and being 'seen' as the expert in your niche means being 'found' via Google and all other search engines.

You may be thinking, 'Ahhh, why do I have to think about this?'. The answer is simple. Often when we're looking for experts, we go online and Google relevant keywords in order to track someone down. For instance, if we urgently need an electrician to solve a problem and we live in Greenwich, we will likely go online and Google 'electrician in Greenwich'. If you're an electrician in Greenwich, wouldn't you want to be the one who appears first on a search? Then, when the potential customer clicks through to your website, your personal brand needs to kick in. You get about 30 seconds to demonstrate you're an expert.

If your website is basic and looks like all the other electricians' websites in the market, the potential customer might go to the next website. If your website is very personal, perhaps with a video of you on the home page talking about what you do, why you do it, and how you do it for your customer (think back to the work you did in defining your perfect customer avatar), has testimonials, your qualifications and other relevant information, you're going to immediately stand out from others.

The only way you're going to be the electrician who appears on a Google search for 'electrician in Greenwich' is if you've optimised your website for those and other similar keywords. If you haven't then you won't get noticed. In fact, you won't even appear on page one of the search. You may not appear anywhere.

So, after defining our market niche and customer avatar, we must identify the relevant keywords that will attract our potential customer to us when they Google, which they will.

What keywords must you secure to be found for as part of your marketing and positioning strategy?   Your keywords may relate to what you do and where you do it. Search engine optimisation is a complex and fast changing world, so I encourage you to get expert help to support you in identifying the perfect keywords for you and your business, and how you integrate them into your online presence to be found for them.

Writing Your Best Résumé

You may be thinking, 'I own a business. I don't need a résumé'. But you never know when it might be useful. You might be asked to give a keynote speech at an industry event and the organisers will need your bio for the programme. You may need it if you're tendering for a piece of work where presenting your credentials is an important part of the process. Depending on your industry there will be specific advice available to help you perfect your résumé but from the point of view of personal branding there are a few tips that will help you to rise to the top of the pile.

Tailor your résumé to the person or company you are sending it to each time. This takes time but is well worth the investment as you can make sure that everything you include is relevant to the reader. Always research that person or company thoroughly so that you can connect with them. It seems obvious but many people skim this part and so just showing you care enough to find out about them will go a long way to helping your cause.

Instead of listing your work experience and accomplishments separately, match them together. This brings your résumé to life and means that people will be much more likely to notice the value of your accomplishments. The same goes for your attributes, for example being a team player or having leadership skills. It will have much more impact if you can illustrate these attributes through examples rather than simply stating that you possess them.

Often, the most effective use of a résumé can be when you've made personal contact beforehand and someone knows to look out for it. You may have made contact through a networking event or through LinkedIn, or an associate who has made introductions for you. This is a golden opportunity to show not only your excellent and relevant experience, but bring together the elements of your personal branding such as your style (page 87), your online presence (page 105) and links to any publications or content you have contributed to. Do you need to create a résumé? If so, please download my free résumé template at: www.smallbusinesshugesuccess.com/personalbranding

As a business person, you must also be visible on LinkedIn. That's a résumé too. In chapter 6 we talk more about how to effectively create your LinkedIn profile so you correctly position yourself as the go-to expert in your niche, while optimising it for keywords so you get found on LinkedIn.

As you use the tools in this book to develop your personal brand, your résumé, like your LinkedIn profile, becomes a shop window for who you are, what you do and how you stand out. It's a great exercise to spruce up your résumé once a year even if you don't need to send it out for any specific reason. It will help you hone your personal brand, which is organic and evolving, just as you are.

Elevator Pitch

A friend of mine tells the story of getting into the lift at work, only to be face to face with her CEO, who immediately said, 'Hi, what are you doing?' Flustered (it was her first job in London), she replied, 'I'm going to the fifth floor.'

'No, I mean what do you do?'

Now that's someone who needed an elevator pitch! I know, we're back to that old chestnut, 'what do you do?'. Such a seemingly simple question, but wow, it's not easy to have an answer that sounds relaxed, assertive and intriguing all at the same time in just a few seconds. In business we all need elevator pitches, as we're always being asked that question, and we're asked the question at unexpected times – kids' school events, talking to strangers at parties, or on an aeroplane. In order to be memorable and to stand out, we must have a compelling response.

Now that you've identified your audience, your value and what you offer, you can begin to craft your positioning pitch. The key to remember with any pitch or conversation of this kind is that it always needs to be about the other person, even if they are seemingly asking about you. How does what you do relate to them? If it doesn't in any way then it's a conversation non-starter. In business, your pitch is your opportunity to tell a mini story, rather than reel off a list of the things that you do. No one wants to hear you're an estate agent, but everyone wants to know if you can help them figure out how to buy a house or sell theirs without the standard headaches. Start off with 'I'm an accountant,' and watch people's eyes glaze over, but tell a story of how your expertise really helped someone or a company substantially reduce their tax bill (legally) and people will listen.

So, think about how you can personalise what you do. How does it help people or enhance their lives?

Here's another way of thinking about it. When people ask you the question, 'What do you do' if you answer with something like, 'I'm an accountant' or 'I'm a lawyer' or 'I own a catering company', then you're not really telling them what you do. You're telling them 'what you are'. There's a big difference. What you do versus what you are. Always remember that 'what you do' is the difference you make in the lives of others, and 'what you are' is the recognisable title you have in doing that work. At the start no-one wants to hear your title as that's boring and a potential conversation stopper. Make it easy for the listener to say, 'wow, tell me some more' after you've told them what you do in an interesting and perhaps slightly cryptic way.

By way of example, if I were to say to someone I meet that 'I'm a business coach', often their eyes would roll as business coaches are a dime a dozen in the market now. But when I respond by saying 'I guide business owners and entrepreneurs to achieve profitable and scalable growth and extraordinary success, as they define it', then the person listening always asks the question, 'Wow, how do you do that?' and 'What type of clients do you work with?' It's a conversation starter... and I can then gear my response to their situation so I'm relatable to their business.

The key is to leave them asking for more so that you can converse, and later swap contact details and follow up the conversation.

Here are five examples for you to ponder as you create your own enticing pitch.

1. **Boring:** I'm a chartered accountant and I do year end accounts and tax returns for small businesses.

   Enticing: I work with small business owners who have a turnover of over $1M. I ensure they have sufficient capital to support their growth aspirations, and that they benefit from all the business and tax reduction schemes that are legally available so they maximise their profit and minimise tax paid each year.

2. **Boring:** I'm a property investment consultant and I help new investors get into the property market.

   Enticing: I'm a property investment consultant and I guide inexperienced property investors to buy rental properties across the UK that generate yields of 10 percent per annum, using other people's money. One client bought 10 properties in one year, and now enjoys passive income of $50K per annum.

3. **Boring:** I'm a florist.

   Enticing: I'm a florist and I specialise in creating the most stunning and memorable bouquets for weddings, so that the day is even more special for the happy couple. My work has been featured in three of the UK's leading bridal magazines.

4. **Boring:** I'm a builder and I do new builds and renovation work.

   Enticing: I'm a builder and I specialise in building bespoke homes for discerning home owners. Typically the houses I build cost $5-10M and are built to the highest specification. One of the houses I built won a national architectural and building award.

5. **Boring:** I own a gym in Greenwich.

   Enticing: Along with my personal training team, we inspire and guide our clients at my gym to achieve their health and fitness goals. Our speciality is helping men and women safely muscle up through weight training to compete in natural body-building competitions.

Summary

When you take the time to understand yourself and really think about who you are, it naturally becomes easier to more clearly position your personal brand and your pitch. In today's business world it isn't always enough to be good at what we do, how we are perceived is equally important, and when it comes to getting our foot in the door, paramount. In this chapter we've looked at how you need to identify who you are serving, know exactly what their needs are and offer the best, easiest, most convenient and personable solution available. We've introduced keywords so that you can begin to match up your promise with your online copy and search terms. When you position yourself effectively, the potential for success immediately opens up, and as we will explore in the next chapter, developing your personal brand allows you to then really connect with people and not only be remembered but asked for time and time again.

ACTION

What is the market niche that you are serving?

_____

_____

_____

_____

What is your unique value proposition (UVP) for your market niche?

_____

_____

_____

What are some of the key words you want to capture for your marketing and search engine optimisation?

_____

_____

_____

_____

How will you answer the question: 'What do you do?' – what's your enticing pitch?

_____

_____

_____

_____

Sir Richard Branson

'Life is a helluva lot more fun if you say yes rather than no.'

For Sir Richard Branson's 65th birthday he requested 65 challenges from readers of his blog that he would complete over the course of the year #CHALLENGERICHARD. From being challenged to sit for 65 minutes and do nothing but stare out the window like when he was a kid to tweeting 65 business lessons to writing a letter to his grandchildren, the whole idea and the resulting challenges sum up Richard Branson so well. He will launch himself into new things with such energy and enthusiasm that even if something doesn't work out he never regrets trying and learning and moving on to the next frontier, which now even includes space tourism.

Branson was born in Blackheath, London, in 1950. From an early age at school he struggled due to dyslexia; the famous observation from his headteacher was that he would either end up in prison or become a millionaire (make that billionaire). His entrepreneurial spirit was there from his teens; at 18 he published the magazine 'Student' and then started to sell records by mail order at 20 years old. This became a store that became a recording studio and Virgin Records. By 23 years he had signed The Rolling Stones and The Sex Pistols and was a millionaire.

Virgin is now an umbrella company for over 400 companies, from trains to planes, hotels, mobile phones and is now venturing into deep sea and space tourism with Virgin Galactic. In 2000, Richard Branson was knighted in honour of his services to entrepreneurship, and he truly is the epitome of an entrepreneur. He moves fast both in business and in life, never afraid to try something, to fail and pick himself up and move on quickly to the next project that excites him.

Branson's personal brand is there in every fabric of his being. Not only does he want to put the first tourists into space, but he became the first person to cross the Atlantic in a hot air balloon in 1987 and the oldest man to kite surf across the English Channel at 61 years old. He has always worked hard and played hard, the owner of a private island in the British Virgin Islands, where he wines and dines the rich and famous as well as other entrepreneurs and business partners, and mavericks like himself.

Like other highly successful and personally branded individuals, Branson is honest about who he is and consistent. Perhaps that's why people often can't help but like him even in the face of the lavish displays of monetary success. He champions young people, and in particular those who are dyslexic like himself, he gives a great deal of his time to mentoring and his money to charity. When the SpaceShip Two crashed, killing one test pilot and injuring another, he didn't flinch from showing his emotion and talking about what happened. He openly faltered, and then in true Branson style he flew straight to the test site to be with the project team, who urged him to keep going with it. As a modern-day pioneer and business explorer he has the ability to learn fast from failure, pick everyone up from the floor with his drive and enthusiasm and keep moving forward, always forward.

As a business leader, Branson the person is highly visible online and in the media. He has written a number of bestselling books, including *Losing My Virginity* and *Business Stripped Bare*. Whether he writes every word or not, his blog on www. virgin.com is a generous insight into the mind and life of an entrepreneur. One post might be a letter written from Branson to a child who sent him their design for a new airplane, encouraging their creativity and innovation, another might be a description of when a friend of Branson's kite surfed off the roof of his house into the sea at Necker Island (his private Caribbean island). There are pictures of Branson giving a speech next to photos of him in shorts, tanned and smiling with friends. He's nearly always smiling in pictures, and never constrained by overly smart clothes. He really seems to be completely excited by life and what it has offered him, or perhaps more what he has gone out and found for himself.

Chapter 5

Personalisation

'Your only obligation in any lifetime is to be true to yourself.'
– Richard Bach

People connect with us when we are real and not some 'plastic fantastic' image we create of ourselves. How many times have you observed another person and wondered if they are really being themselves or if they are 'putting it on' for the audience or you?

Once upon a time, often that's the way it was. Famous people had their public persona, and often the real person only came out with their nearest and dearest. Rumours circulated about those people and who they 'really' were. There was a disconnect between the true person and the image they created. In our deepest heart of hearts, I think we know when someone is not being real. If we listen, our intuition tells us what we need to know. Often it encourages us to keep away from those people. Intuitively, we don't trust them... yet we don't always know why (at first).

Personalisation is about being proud of who you are, the stories and scars you have, the way you look, the way you speak. Personalisation is showing everyone you in all your uniqueness. It's about accepting yourself as you are with all your strengths and imperfections. You might be thinking that we must hide our imperfections from everyone. Until recently, I'd have agreed with you as that's what I did. I didn't think anyone would really be interested in some of the challenges of my business and life's journey. How wrong I was!

In fact, I've learnt that by sharing all that, by allowing myself to be vulnerable with others, rather than being a weakness vulnerability is an incredible strength. People warm to us more if we are prepared to be open, honest and raw. They don't want perfection as they believe they can't measure up to that. With our imperfections, we are just like them. Human. When we are human, we create an emotional connection with others. We build respect. We build trust. We build admiration. Sometimes we even build love.

In building our personal brand, there are three or four areas we must think about in relation to personalisation. They are:

- Your Story
- Your Voice
- Your Style
- Your Title (sometimes)

What's Your Story?

The simplest and perhaps the most powerful way to articulate your personal brand is through the art of storytelling.

Stories have the ability to paint a picture with words, tapping into the imagination of the listener or reader and allowing you to connect with them. The stories you tell will show whether or not you are a team player, have initiative, purpose; they enable you to stand out and be memorable, and to show your human side.

Your story isn't your entire life's autobiography. It's a snapshot that gives the perfect illustration in a specific situation. For example, when I guide entrepreneurs and business owners on how to maximise their profits, it helps when I tell them about my own experiences growing businesses to create multi-million dollar revenues and profits. Business success is not linear, it's not a straight line from start up to success. It's a long journey of twists and turns, curveballs and more. I often share my experiences in business dealing with not enough clients, too many clients, clients who don't pay, loads of cash in the bank and often no cash in the bank (especially at month end when salaries and monthly bills were due), high and low performing staff, supporting a staff member who tried to commit suicide, another who was assaulted... winning profitable contracts and losing them. You get the picture. I think I've dealt with just about everything business can throw at us.

The healthy food author Ella Woodward has made a massive success from the story she tells of being chronically ill and curing her symptoms through food. Emma, the fertility expert from earlier, often tells the story of when she first had acupuncture and what a great impact it had on her, releasing a dam of grief.

The more we share our story, the more relevant we are to our audience. The more they think, 'Wow, they really know what I'm going through'. That builds trust and respect.

If you are reading this book, then it's almost 100% likely that you are either already working in an area of business of personal interest to you, or that you are looking to evolve your business and your personal brand to do just that. When you begin to articulate the personal stories behind why you do what you do, they add to your credibility, show that you are genuine and have personal experience in your subject.

Even in an interview setting, storytelling transforms a formal list of experience into rich illustrations of why they should employ you. Always have some professional experiences ready to talk about; what you did, how you felt, why it was such a great outcome for everyone involved.

And while you might not want to talk about your 'failures' in an interview to pitch for funding or a contract, these can also turn into brilliant stories that actually highlight how you are willing to learn from experiences. The now CEO of one of the biggest publishing companies in the United Kingdom was known for telling employees about his disastrous books; they worked so well because they were funny, showed his human side and encouraged all the commissioning editors to be brave with their commissioning, because for all his flops he had many more winners because he was willing to take a chance on authors he passionately believed in.

You might be known for your honesty and integrity, people might talk about how exceptional your customer service is in that you and your business go beyond the call of duty; all this is your personal brand working hard for you. Your challenge is to then know how to bring brand 'you' alive when it comes to the next business interview or meeting.

'Be so good they can't ignore you.' - Steve Martin

3 steps to great stories

1. The first step is being purposeful with your personal brand stories. Make sure you share the stories according to the situation. There's no point in sharing a story that's about bending rules and getting outcomes if the opportunity or project requires you to be a stickler for rules. Skim through your experiences both personal and work related to find stories that provide you with a sense of purpose that is relevant. What are the needs of the other person and how can you show your experience with meeting those needs, with being a solution provider? Listen during the meeting, be willing to go with the flow of the conversation and use the best, most appropriate story rather than being like a politician and giving the same answers, whatever the questions. Think of how little trust we have for politicians when we spot that strategy.

2. Secondly you need to use stories that have concrete evidence. If you have figures such as 'improved response time by 15 percent', then provide evidence that supports this story and what impact is had. Make sure you always use both concrete data and stories. The combination of the two will provide you with a compelling case when it comes to contracting you or making a business deal that means you are chosen over your competitors.

3. Thirdly, you need to ensure your stories are authentic, true and accurate. Stories that are real and in need of no exaggeration or embellishment are the most impactful and memorable. If you are interviewing to win a contract alongside six other candidates who are all equally as well qualified, what will make you stand out? It's the connection and impact you make with the experience you share

during that meeting or interview. When we are authentic, we are at our most open. When we show our vulnerability, we are being real. Being real gives you your best chance of making the right deals or landing your dream contract. And even if it's not meant to be this time, you know you put your best and real self forward. Equally, presenting your own personal and relevant stories when pitching to potential clients to win work will endear you to them. You won't always win the work but you will be held in high regard for your honesty and authenticity, rather than for delivering a 'plastic fantastic' pitch, as often occurs in some industries.

Your Voice

Voice has a critical role to play in personal branding. It can amplify or detract from your personal brand. As motivational speaker, Les Brown rightly says: 'When you open your mouth, you tell the world who you are.' Voice reveals personality. It also reflects emotions. We can hear it when someone feels happy, sad, or angry. People pick up what's happening for you through your voice. We cannot hide. Voice is the vehicle to the soul. Therefore, you can use your voice to your advantage. It can support you towards standing out and becoming influential and branded.

In her powerful and thought provoking book, *Influence Through Voice*, Cynthia Zhai discusses how we can harness the power of our voice to gain respect, establish authority and to leave an impact. That's personal branding.

Cynthia Zhai suggests the factors that detract from our voice include: pitch (too high or low), speed (speaking too fast or slow), nasality (too much sound coming through the nose so the voice sounds 'whiney or twangy'), mumbling, harshness (where the voice sounds sharp, shrill and unpleasant), and monotony (where the voice is boring!).

While I'm not suggesting that to create a personal brand we must all be public speakers, we must look at our voice as a tool in the arsenal that can help us to stand out more.

Think about people you know who are branded. Think about their voice. What do they sound like? Think about how easy it is to listen to Oprah Winfrey's voice, how core it is to her personal brand and success. Think about people in your industry who give great presentations as opposed to those who you might listen less attentively to. When you combine good stories with a relaxed, clear, timely delivery, you give yourself the best chance to be heard and remembered for what you say and how you say it.

Personal Style

> 'Style is very personal. It has nothing to do with fashion.'
> – Ralph Lauren

Your personal style is your personal brand image and will help you to stand out and be memorable, from your appearance to your website and the tone of your communication. Elon Musk is known as the world's coolest CEO. A self-made billionaire, he also likes to hang out with his brother, Kimbal, co-founder of a non-profit organisation The Kitchen Community. Everyone wants to hang out with Elon, and you'll seldom see him without one of his trademark jackets. For Mark Zuckerberg, it's the hoodies and grey tee-shirts, and for Steve Jobs it was the glasses and black sweaters.

What's your style? It doesn't have to be crazy, but first impressions are often created by appearances and so if you have a recognisable style then it helps people remember you and who you are. Whatever your business or industry, it's possible to use style as a way to strengthen your brand.

Plumbers who turn up in smart work clothes (that fit!) make a great impression. Chefs with clean jackets. Your style should fit what you do but also allow you to show your personality and feel your confidence. It may be a flash of colour in your lapel, your shoes. Or maybe you're like my friend, Deri Llewellyn-Davies, The Strategy Man. He's well known for wearing highly tailored three piece suits with a twist. Deri's suits are part of his personal brand.

My friend, Brad Burton, is a well known motivational speaker and the founder of 4Networking, a leading business networking organisation in the United Kingdom. He has a fascinating and scar-filled background that he shares to inspire others. His wardrobe for all his work is jeans and a tee-shirt that displays his personal motto, 'Help Many. Hurt Few. Live Life.'

There is no one way to image yourself. A small detail will catch the eye. If you're unsure of your style, get professional help with an image consultant. What really suits you? What are you wearing when you both look your best and 'feel' yourself?

You set the tone with your appearance, and this is something you can then use across all your communication platforms. So whether someone is glancing at you at an industry event or landing on your website or LinkedIn profile, they will begin to recognise you. This can be a great way for people to feel they are getting to know you and therefore be more likely to approach you or make a step towards doing business with you.

Mood boards

Mood boards are used by image consultants to help work out which colours and style suit you and your brand. You can begin to do this yourself by looking at the colours of your wardrobe and the style of your home. Go through some magazines and pull out images that appeal to you. Pin them all to a board and you'll soon get a sense of the colours and tone that you might want to use for your website and across your online presence.

You can also think about the characteristics that will influence your style and image. For example, are you more casual than smart, sophisticated, friendly, humorous or authoritative? These characteristics can help you choose the fonts and images for your website, business card etc. Even a seemingly effortless, casual style takes thought and effort to implement well. I know a couple who spent months planning their wedding to really suit their style, which on the day felt like the most relaxed beach gathering but was actually made by all the little details like the wild flowers in every corner and around the cake, the brown paper menus, the mismatched chairs and recycled wooden long tables, candles, lanterns and Edison lights everywhere that were lit as dusk fell. What are the details that make your style?

Meeting people in person

In today's digital age sometimes we forget how important it is to shape our personal brand in person as well as online. But these are the moments that can provide real trigger points in business and life in general. And yes, first impressions count a great deal.

Take any occasion that you may be invited to, you get dressed and get there on time and so have an opportunity to mingle with the crowd. And it is in just a few seconds with only a brief glance that an unfamiliar stranger will go some way towards evaluating your appearance, and in turn what type of person they think you are. If you are a valuable team player who brings out the best in people, you might not have a natural style that will shout out from the crowd, but if people can see the very best parts of your personality in your appearance, they will feel as though they know you even before you speak.

I have a client who used to walk into a room of people believing she was invisible and that no one would come and talk to her. And so, consistently, nobody did. What you think becomes your reality! It turns out that she didn't think she wasn't interesting or would have anything relevant or impactful to say, quite the opposite, but she had always believed that she could just never make an impactful first impression with her appearance. With a little coaching, she realised that if she made a conscious effort to wear the best clothes she had that also felt like her personality, i.e. someone who could happily live at the beach for the rest of her days, she could make exactly the right kind of first impression.

'I was invited to speak at a seminar. It was a beautiful summer's day and so I decided to wear my favourite cotton dress. It's fitted and covers the shoulders so I knew it was appropriate, but it's also the colour of a deep blue sky, it has an element of nature and the outdoors just like me! I felt well dressed and comfortable in myself at the same time, and the first thing the host said to me when I went up to speak was, 'Wow, you look lovely today'. Maybe it's a coincidence but I received an avalanche of positive feedback about my contribution to the seminar that has since blossomed into some fruitful professional relationships.'

Nicoletta Adda is a London based personal style expert who recommends that you ask yourself two simple but powerful questions:

- What do people see when I walk into a room?
- Does my image communicate my personal and professional best?

However much we know that it's what on the inside that truly counts with people, what's on the outside does make an impression and rightly or wrongly conveys something about us. It doesn't mean you have to be the most smartly dressed person in the room. A chef I know was at a fancy cookbook launch and said the most memorable person there was a producer from Cornwall who grows the most incredible micro herbs and edible flowers. He was barefoot all night, which perfectly matches his personality and his brand as someone who is completely immersed in nature.

The important thing is that your personal brand and style doesn't alienate but rather invites your audience to connect with you. What lies beneath is the core of what you do and who you are, but when you match up the outward impression you give with those things then you'll attract more of the right people who will appreciate and value what you offer.

ACTION

Give yourself a style check, from your wardrobe to the stationary you use. What is your style? Do you feel you're making the best possible impression when you walk into a room?

_____

_____

_____

_____

_____

_____

_____

_____

_____

_____

What style role models can you think of where you can evolve their ideas to suit you?

_____

_____

_____

_____

Look at how your style can be more consistent across your online platforms, from your website to social media profiles. What are some of the ideas you want to consider? Remember to use the same avatar for each (and a really good one), think about the fonts and colours you are using.

_____

_____

_____

_____

_____

Your Title

Some people are able to augment their personal brand with a catchy business title. My friend Deri Llewellyn-Davies is known as The Strategy Man. He owns the website domain www.thestrategyman.com and he brands himself with this title.

Remember the Burglar Annoyer? That's a title. And it's catchy and memorable. So is my friend who is The Prince of Printing – type this into Google or via LinkedIn and you can meet Ricardo da Corte.

Well known juice advocate, Jason Vale styles himself as the Juice Master and owns www.juicemaster.com to support this title.

Are you able to turn what you do into a fun and memorable title that becomes part of your personal brand? If you can, you'll be remembered for it.

Have some fun

Too many of us take our business too seriously. How about having some fun with yours?

Here are some examples that might make you smile. These people say the following when asked what they do. Their responses certainly beg another question, perhaps something like, 'what does that mean?' – and then the conversation starts.

- 'I take the SH out of IT' (he's an IT support consultant)
- 'I legally expose you' (he sells promotional merchandise)
- 'I make you look good on paper' (she's a printer)
- 'I keep your head above water' (he's a plumber)
- 'I record history' (she's a photographer)

...and my favourite because it's really clever... 'I'm a skeleton creator' (he's a structural engineer).

So now it's over to you! Can you be more memorable by having an interesting, perhaps slightly cryptic business title or in response to the chestnut question, to help stand you out from the crowd? If so, perhaps you can trademark it or at least buy the domain name for it. It's the little extras that help you to stand out in your niche.

Business Cards

This small piece of card can go a long way to reinforcing your personal brand image, but if you go for a cheap option also be aware that it may create a less than favourable early impression. The good news is that simple works best for business cards. Use a comfortable to read size font and plenty of white space. If you are self-employed or own your business then you'll include your company logo, email, telephone, website and social media handles. Either leave the reverse side blank or use a professional quality image that reflects your personal brand.

Remember, if you're able to develop a creative title, then use that on your business card too.

Presenting Your Personal Brand

Your brand needs to be there in your pitches, when you speak on the telephone, in front of one person or a whole room. It will help you to engage and connect with your audience so that you offer them the solution to their needs. Presentations, workshops or webinars can all be golden opportunities to develop and build your personal brand. Successful TED speakers have gone on to write bestselling books based on their 18 minute presentations, and conversely, authors have boosted the sales of their books massively through speaking appearances. Whatever industry you are a part of, if you can develop the skill of speaking and presenting your ideas well, this will catapult your recognition factor upwards.

Your public image becomes even more critical when you're addressing a large group. It's a fact that people generally only remember and retain four percent of any content that is presented to them in the form of speeches or discussions. They will, however, remember 100 percent how they were feeling about it.

Your content is still important, as you want that four percent takeaway message to be both powerful and useful to your audience, so they are more likely to come back for more and tell everyone else how great you are. But your style is what will make you memorable.

Facts tell, stories sell

We come back to sharing stories again. Telling a story is an excellent way to make your presentations absorbing, however large or small your audience. Stories allow you to interact with your audience, they are more memorable than facts and figures, and if you tell a good enough story then it will be passed on, further increasing your personal presence within your industry or with your customers.

The tricky part is that if you're going to tell a story, you need to make it a good one. Listening to boring or irrelevant stories is a turn off for us all. And relevance is essential. Think about when you have been in a seminar or a group conference and someone has taken up 10 minutes of precious time with a hilarious but off-the-point anecdote. They might deliver a brilliant story, but timing and relevance is all important here.

Remember, your examples need to be:

- Purposeful
- Authentic
- To the point

If you have been asked to put together a presentation or you are creating one from scratch from your own idea, always look for whatever it is about the subject that you really care about. This will immediately make your presentation more absorbing as there will be the added layer of passion beneath the content. You can think of a presentation as being a bit like a cake, when you have a story layered with information you make the best combination. Always try to frame your presentation as a journey for the audience, for example:

- Introduce yourself and your subject succinctly
- Present a problem (the pain) relevant to your audience
- Present the outcome when the problem has been solved (the gain)
- Describe your search for the solution and your background 'Aha' moment – when you solved the problem
- Share the solution in a way that's informative and memorable for the audience
- Give the audience actionable steps they can follow to implement your solution

- Recap the benefits of your audience implementing your solution
- Close the presentation with an inspiring ending and thank the audience for listening

Being memorable

To give absorbing presentations you need to be present with your audience and what you are saying. It doesn't matter if you are nervous, it matters that you look people in the eye, give your best inner smile and believe in the power of your words. To help with nerves, before you go on stage, remember to breathe deeply for a couple of minutes. Nerves are natural and it's really okay to show vulnerability, it's an attractive quality. Stand in a relaxed but centred position, upright but not as though you are set in stone. Let your hands do a little of the talking. A good tip during your presentation is to imagine that you are breathing half way to your audience, that you are meeting in the middle. Your energy will draw people towards you, they will lean in to listen. Pick say five random people (or more if the group is large) in the audience and make eye contact with these people every so often (go for friendly faces); it's amazing how this helps your entire audience to connect with you. And remember to be consistent with your tone and style so that others instantly have a sense of recognition.

Summary

How you present yourself, your ideas or your business can have a huge impact on how people perceive you, i.e. your personal brand.

This isn't about who can shout the loudest, it is about people having a really good sense of you and what you represent so that they remember you when they need your product or services, or so that they look out for your events and workshops or just have to come up and ask you where you get your glasses. Your style, your tone, your voice and your stories are all a reflection of you, and so when you tap into your authentic self it immediately becomes apparent and attractive to others. The next step is to use your own personal style and content consistently across the right platforms to grow your audience or customer base. So let's do just that.

ACTION

Think about a topic you are passionate about and would love to share with others.

_____
_____
_____
_____

Drill down to a specific problem that you have found or created a solution for.

_____
_____
_____
_____

Map out the journey of how you got to that moment and then what it is.

_____
_____
_____
_____

Practise the above as a 10 minute presentation to build your confidence.

Oprah Winfrey

'Turn your wounds into wisdom.'

Oprah Winfrey by far is one of the most powerfully branded individuals alive today. She has a magazine whose cover features her face each month, her Book Club sends books instantly to the top of the bestseller lists, her own book *Make the Connection* held the #1 spot for months and her network OWN, launched in 2011, while having a rocky start has become another Oprah success story.

Oprah was born to unmarried teenage parents in 1954 in Mississippi. She was meant to be named after a Bible character, Orpah, but a spelling mistake saw Oprah come into the world instead. At 14, she ran away from living with her mother to live in Nashville with her father. She was pregnant and gave birth to a son who died soon after being born. She became an honours student and at 19 was the city's first black TV news correspondent.

In 1976, Oprah moved to Baltimore, where she met her lifelong best friend Gayle King and became co-host on the show People Are Talking, then moved to Chicago to present Chicago AM. In 1985 it was renamed The Oprah Winfrey Show and became the biggest talk show in America.

Oprah is, in Kevin Roberts' words, a true 'lovemark'. As Jennifer Harris and Elwood Watson wrote in *The Oprah Phenomenon*, she transforms viewers into loyal consumers (and is fiercely loyal herself), and more than that they love her as a friend. Oprah's personal brand has been consistent throughout her life and career; she keeps her private life private while at the same time being very honest, open and compassionate. During her shows, and more frequently now her transformational webinars and series, she appears to be transparent, she is the leader who isn't afraid to show her vulnerability. Her viewers have watched her struggles with weight over the years and because she is so genuine, they don't judge her but empathise and feel a part of her journey.

One time Oprah admitted that she had starved herself for weeks to lose weight, and while she looked amazing on the outside had done nothing to address what was going on inside. She immediately began to comfort herself with food and the weight quickly came back on. This kind of admission is why Oprah's brand is so strong and long-lasting. If she weren't willing to open up in this way there would be more distance and therefore less love and loyalty from her viewers. But as it is they are willing to rally around her even when she is questioned. She catapulted the author James Frey to fame when she interviewed him about his book *A Million Little Pieces*. It then turned out much of the book was fiction when Frey had presented it as autobiographical. Oprah was caught up in someone else's lack of authenticity and it threatened to tarnish her own brand, but instead of shunning him she invited him back to the show, confronted him and asked him to apologise to her viewers.

Staying true to her values has proven financially beneficial too. As other daytime talk shows became fixated on negative, trashy stories, Oprah moved the other way. The mission of the show, reflecting Oprah's own personal mission, was to 'be a catalyst for transformation in people's lives'. She was one of the first high profile presenters to create online webinar series, in order to 'be of service' to the viewers and offer deeper layers of teaching than could be contained in a television show.

Oprah's personal brand is so big that there could be a danger of losing the personal touch that made her name in the first place, but as she stays true to herself and her values, her viewers stay true to her. You don't need to fit a mould or follow a fashion. Brand YOU is being you, stay true to yourself and your brand will flourish.

Chapter 6

Platforms

'Personal branding is about managing your name – even if you don't own a business – in a world of misinformation, disinformation, and semi-permanent Google records. Going on a date? Chances are that your 'blind' date has Googled your name. Going to a job interview? Ditto.' – Tim Ferriss

Now that you have taken steps to create your personal brand, you can begin to build on those foundations, amplifying your message and connecting with your community through your brand platforms, both online and in person. It's important to take the time to understand yourself and what you stand for because that sense of identity will give clarity and consistency as you begin to build your online presence, pitch and present to others, create products, content and collaborations.

You need to harness the best avenues available to you for building your profile, both online and in person. Be your own social PR expert, show up at the right events, be on the right social media, listen and then talk to your potential audience. Building your profile not only increases your visibility but it determines what people see.

Online Profile

Often the first thing we do when we meet people in a professional context is Google them. We might even do this before a first meeting, to get a sense of the person. There's a great deal you can do to influence what comes up on that all-important first page of results. If you have a personal website plus an excellent LinkedIn profile, for example, you have the best opportunity to create the first impression that you wish to give, rather than leave it to chance that you show up somewhere on the internet for something that you've done, or that you don't turn up at all.

You can also build your personal brand profile through additional social networking sites such as YouTube, Twitter, Instagram, Google+, Pinterest, Facebook and Snapchat. These are the most popular online marketing platforms at the time of publishing this book. Once you have established yourself on these platforms you can use them to reach more of the right people with your blog or video posts and podcasts, forum comments and products/offerings.

It's really important to note that even if you aren't looking to sell specific products or services online, nor want to be an online marketing personality like many are these days, improving your online presence will have a beneficial effect on your overall reputation and how people perceive you and your value, as the digital world is now very important to personal branding. The more consistent you are across all those platforms, being yourself while also being professional, the more people will feel they can trust you and your brand because they can see exactly what you stand for at the click of a button. Your online presence should reflect and enhance your personal presence. You don't have to be 100 percent squeaky clean, but it's important to be relevant and interesting.

'We all have personal brands and most of us have already left a digital footprint, whether we like it or not. Proper social media use highlights your strengths that may not shine through in an interview or application and gives the world a broader view of who you are. Use it wisely.' – Amy Jo Martin, Renegades Write the Rules

Creating Your Online Profile

Consistency is crucial for helping you build your personal brand, both in person and online. This begins with creating your personal professional profile that you can use across a whole number of different platforms, from your own website to social media sites like LinkedIn, Twitter, Google+, Pinterest, Instagram, Facebook, and any other shiny new tools that appear on the market.

There is such an array of social media to engage with that you could spend all day doing it. I strongly urge you to pick two or three platforms that most resonate with you and your audience, and focus on developing your personal brand on those.

A national study in the US was conducted by BrandYourself to assess how much people are influenced by Google when making choices about who they do business with, as well as who they vote for or even date. They found that 75 percent of adults had searched themselves, and of those, 48 percent had found results they perceived to be negative, while 30 percent found nothing came up at all. Almost half the respondents had searched before doing business with someone, and 45 percent had discovered something which led them not to go ahead. We must attempt to control or at least influence what is seen about us online. The good news is that when you take steps to take care of your personal brand, you can begin to ensure that you not only appear on Google results pages, but for all the right reasons.

Right now, what do people see when they Google your name? Have a go and see what comes up. Are you happy with how quickly you appear and the first sites that come up as links to click through to? Could you improve those sites, whether it's your LinkedIn profile, your company page profile or your personal professional website?

If you want to appear more often on page one of a Google search, then consider these steps to improve Google search results for your name.

- Create a personal professional website with 'your name' in the url (see page 112)
- Ensure you have a LinkedIn profile with vanity url including 'your name' (see page 119)
- Create a Twitter account @yourname (see page 122)
- Along with your personal Facebook page, create a personal Facebook fanpage with 'your name' in the url (see page 125)
- Create a Google+ with vanity url including 'your name'
- Write guest articles and posts on high ranking sites
- Publish a book or ebook through Amazon (see page 156)

Avatar and Cover Shots

Guy Kawasaki, former chief evangelist of Apple and now of the online design service Canva, recommends using the same avatar (headshot) wherever possible to increase recognisability and improve search results for your name at the same time. Use a professional shot if possible, or at least a quality shot where your face is clear, in good light, and you look engaging and approachable.

Your cover shots, often the narrow bands at the top of your profile page, are great for telling a visual story about what you do. Keep it simple and stunning.

If you look me up on any of my social media profiles which are currently Facebook Fanpage (search for AdeleMcLayFan), Instagram and Twitter (both as @AdeleMcLay), LinkedIn, YouTube, Pinterest, and Google+ you will see I use the same photo on each of those platforms. My cover shots are generally similar on all platforms too, although I will change individual cover shots depending on what's important at the time.

Your Bio

Depending on the platform you can decide which part of your bio to display first. Make sure your bio is compelling reading. Keep it punchy and to the point.

Here is an example, Guy Kawasaki's LinkedIn summary:

'Guy possesses an extensive knowledge of innovation, entrepreneurship, social media, and marketing. First and foremost, he is an evangelist. The term comes from a Greek word that means 'bringing the good news.' That's what he does – whether it was the good news of Macintosh or currently the good news of Canva, an online graphics-design firm. He aligns with companies and causes that empowers people, democratizes technology, and makes the world more of a meritocracy.

In addition to his work at Canva, he is a writer (thirteen books), speaker, startup advisor, trustee of the Wikimedia Foundation (Wikipedia), Mercedes brand ambassador, and executive fellow at the Haas School of Business at UC Berkeley. Specialties: innovation, entrepreneurship, marketing, and social media.'

And take a look at my own summary profile on LinkedIn:

'I guide businesses – owners and entrepreneurs – to achieve extraordinary & sustainable business growth & success. I've been a business growth and peak performance consultant/mentor for over 20 years. I'm a Chartered Accountant by qualification too. I'm also a personal branding strategist, helping you (the person) to stand head and shoulders above your competitors in your market.

I get results with you! Big ones! Fast! How? Together we'll develop high growth strategies that drive your business success. To support your business success, my areas of business expertise include: leadership, strategy, personal branding, marketing, sales, finance, team, customer excellence, personal development.'

Your Brand Mantra

The only extra thing you need now is a short (easier said than done) mantra or purpose that you can use directly beneath your name. Again this needs to be memorable and ideally communicate your main purpose. For me, I have: 'Alive. Passionate. Extraordinary. In business and life.' across my various online platforms, business cards and resources. It sums up my purpose to guide people take the steps they need to create a profitable and successful business that is a part of an extraordinary life, as they define it. That sense of balance is important to me personally and so it infuses all my work with clients. It's what helps make me stand out.

Brand strap lines are an art in themselves, so don't get caught up with trying to come up with the perfect line if that's stopping you from getting your bio online. It may come to you as you are developing your online presence, just keep playing around with it and asking yourself, what do others get out of what you do or who you are? Asking this question often is one of the best ways to keep checking in on your personal brand.

Say you were a financial adviser, for example. Simply saying 'financial adviser' after your name isn't going to help you stand out or attract the specific types of people that you are particularly good at helping. Perhaps you 'help families plan finances for a secure future' or you have a way of making the language of finance clear for anyone who thinks they don't understand it, 'finance jargon translator'. Play around with this, looking again at your key strengths, your personality and the characteristics and needs of your core audience.

Professional/Business Personal Website

A well constructed business focused personal website is a valuable platform for developing your personal brand and profile. This allows you to create your personal professional logo or 'look' (this could simply be a font that suits your style) that you can use on your business card, in presentations and various other digital profiles. It provides instant access to your portfolio and also allows you to have a personalised email address. It makes it easier for people to quickly find and contact you, and just as your appearance gives you the opportunity to make a great first impression in person, your website can wow people when they first find you online.

A professional personal website doesn't have to be expensive, but it does need to have the following:

A url that includes your name – if you have an unusual name then you might be able to secure www.yourname.com through a domain registration service. Do it today! If your name has already been taken, then think of how to incorporate it in a simple alternative. If you're based in the UK, check if .co.uk is available, add your middle initial, your profession, keeping it as simple as possible.

Your purpose – this will immediately show people what you do and who you are.

Call to action – you need to give people a great reason to sign up and give you permission to communicate with them (ideally through email), either for updates or some excellent information you have, so that they become part of your online community. This is where they give you their name and email address in exchange for something – a report, a free Skype consultation, anything that is relevant and valuable to your desired target audience.

About you – you can use the bio from page 109 here. You might want to start with a paragraph of description before detailing your career experience.

Examples of your work – Projects, campaigns, illustrations of what you do and can do.

Testimonials or reviews – Referrals are the backbone of personal branding, and so if you do a great job for someone, don't be shy about asking politely if they would write a few words as a review.

What you offer – Your website is your shop window, even if you don't take transactions directly through it. Be ultra clear about what it is that you offer – this is your opening pitch.

Up-to-date blog entries – Does everybody need a blog? This one is up to you, because if you decide to have a blog then you need to consistently post once a week as a minimum. Your entries don't need to be long, between 500-800 words is optimum. It's definitely an excellent way to be seen as a specialist or thought leader in your field over time, plus search engines will boost your site rankings if you have a regular blog and if it is appropriately optimised for keywords. If blogs are old news in your area, would videos or podcasts make more of a splash?

Videos – Social marketing experts are saying that video is the way of the future in that many of us like to consume our content visually. Given the vast volumes of videos that are uploaded to YouTube each day, there's probably some truth in that assertion.

As Google owns YouTube, if you are creating videos for your personal YouTube channel, you will boost your rankings on Google with your videos. If you are also putting those videos onto your website fully keyword optimised, then you get a double Google ranking boost.

The algorithms that Google uses to rank content change almost daily and it is a super duper secret as to what and how they rank. Regardless, it's widely accepted that the more platforms you are placing correctly optimised content on, the more easily you'll be found via Google for your keywords.

Clear contact details – Make it as easy as possible for people to get in touch with you.

Links to your social media profiles – LinkedIn, Twitter, Facebook, Instagram, Google+, Pinterest to name the big ones. This is really important. Place your social media links in a range of locations on your website to continually remind people reading your website that you are on social media. It saves them scrolling around your site to find your links should they wish to connect with you on social media. My own website www.adelemclay.com is a good example of this. I have links to my social media at various places on my website to make connecting with me on social media easy.

Tips for your website

When creating your website, go for a hosting package that works easily with Wordpress as your platform. Not only does Wordpress come with an amazing array of free or low-cost plug-ins such as contact forms, and integration with mail list services like Mailchimp, it also means that if you want to adapt and make changes to your site in the future you aren't wedded to one designer and their bespoke website design and supporting technology.

Shop around for your url and hosting package as prices vary considerably.

If you go for the Wordpress platform option, then you will also have good options when it comes to designers. As I said a personal website needn't be expensive to look smart and attractive. Check out Theme Foundry (www.thethemefoundry.com) for a treasure trove of design themes that you can explore. Then you can ask a website designer who specialises in adapting themes to adapt your favourite according to exactly what you need. This is a less expensive option than starting from scratch, and often with even better results.

Ask for feedback on your site from people who are your target audience (not your loved ones) in exchange for your expertise. Is it clear what you stand for, what do they remember from the site, did your call to action work?

Keep your website up-to-date with recent projects, new testimonials, press pieces and blog articles. This will not only raise your site in the Google search rankings, but will make a much stronger impression on visitors.

Check how quickly your site loads. Google doesn't like slow sites, so if yours takes a couple of seconds or more to load, ask your website designer to optimise the site for quicker loading.

Beginner's SEO (Search Engine Optimisation)

There are entire books and many courses devoted to SEO. If you're just starting out with building your online presence I can offer some simple tips that will boost your rankings without giving you a headache!

If you update your website regularly and ensure it's super quick to load then you've already taken a couple of excellent steps to making it search engine friendly. The other crucial thing you need to do is use keywords.

Keywords are those words and more often phrases that people use to find sites through search engines like Google, Bing and Yahoo. Without sounding like a repetitive robot, you can improve your rankings by making sure that your site is keyword rich so that when users enter a query into Google, your site begins to rise to the top of the organic (non paid) results.

The main reasons we enter a word or phrase into a search engine is that we want an answer to a question, a solution to a problem or a piece of information. A useful exercise is therefore to imagine yourself as your target market and write down questions or things they might be looking for online that would lead them to you and the answers, information or solutions that you can provide. These may be location based, especially for service based searches, for example 'private chef in Dorset' or 'acupuncture for fertility in southeast London'.

Search Phase	Answer/solution on my website

When you have decided on the phrases you wish to focus on, you need to make sure these appear in your website in various ways:

- In the url of a web page on your website
- As close to the beginning of the title of a page or blog post as possible
- In a prominent place near the top of the page
- In the alternative text for any images

- Two to three times in the text of the page
- In the tags and meta description

The other best way to improve your SEO is to have other reputable and high ranking websites link to yours, i.e. you need a link building strategy. Here are some of the ways you can build links:

- Guest blogs and articles on high-ranking sites
- Sign up to relevant professional associations (only those which are highly reputable in your field)
- Come together with others in your industry who have different skills and share links
- Engage with relevant blogs. Don't comment just to put your own website url but if there is an option to add it with your name then go ahead
- If you have a great freebie then offer it to relevant sites
- Be newsworthy and 'useworthy' and then people will want to share your posts on their own sites and social media

All this can seem daunting, but if you want to stand out from the crowd you need to be willing to put in the work! Once you are up and running and understand how to check the keywords and metadata on your site or blog, it soon becomes an automatic part of updating and posting. When you have multiple online profiles, you can create an editorial calendar so that you dedicate a little time every week to your online presence. If you take the time and effort to do it well, the ROI will skyrocket.

I Have 'Bad' Content That Needs To Be Buried

Bad news, you have content that's unflattering about you, or your profile is matching the search results of an ex-con or someone in your industry trying to use your name for their own benefit. Regrettably, you can't really remove results from search engines.

However, you do have some options, all it is not lost.

- The only way you can 'BURY', negative content is by piling positive links over it. Site owners will not be asked to remove the content, since the law is on their side for keeping it up and even if you manage to get them to remove it, it will still be in Google' archives. Luckily, there's a solution for you. All you have to do is create as many profiles and links that provide a positive image of you online.

- With many online profiles of yourself depicting a positive image you'll be able to push your negative results down.

LinkedIn Profile

For your professional personal brand, LinkedIn is an essential tool, and provides amazing opportunities for networking with the right people, showcasing your talents and monetising opportunities.

As with anything, you need to 'work the tool' to make it work for you. Just completing your LinkedIn profile and leaving it is generally not enough. Create your profile then use LinkedIn to build your personal brand.

It's easy to set up your profile, and it's well worth spending the time to add as much richness and depth as possible. LinkedIn ranks highly on Google, and so be sure to include the keywords for which you want to be found.

How to create a stellar LinkedIn profile

Many people treat LinkedIn as an online résumé. To a point it is, but it's more. It's not enough just to list your experiences and skills. Your LinkedIn profile must be customer focused, it's really important that you outline what you do in terms of what you do for the benefit of your customer. You can support that by giving examples of work you've done for existing customers. When completing your profile, fill in all the fields available with as much relevant content that you can.

In publications, you can include any free ebooks you have produced.

Tick as many skills as possible, your connections will be asked once in a while if they would like to endorse you, again increasing your visibility. Make sure you display them in the order of priority that are most important for you.

LinkedIn will generate an automatic url for your profile, but you can change this in your account settings to be more recognisable.

Ideally use your name. If your name has already been taken you can add your role (LadyGagaSinger).

If you are just starting with LinkedIn, make sure you have connected with as many people you already know as possible. It's important to get to +500 connections otherwise LinkedIn displays exactly how many connections you have. Fewer than +500 is frowned upon by the active LinkedIn community. Once you have a great profile (including +500 connections), you will notice that increasing numbers of people not only view your profile but request a connection.

My profile on LinkedIn is complete and a good example of what yours should look like (see Adèle McLay). Take a look and use it as a reference tool as you develop or evolve yours. You can connect with me too, if you'd like. Just let me know that you've read this book when you seek to connect with me.

Building your personal branding using LinkedIn

Your profile is done. What next? If you do nothing, then all that will happen is that you will come up on searches if someone is looking for someone with your expertise, so long as your profile is optimised for the keywords you want to be found for.

Building your personal brand on LinkedIn includes writing LinkedIn Pulse articles (you can repurpose blogs from your website to achieve this), and posting relevant content onto your LinkedIn profile. Joining groups is a great way to network with your target market too. Remember to join the groups where your target audience or potential customer is hanging out and networking. Don't join groups where your competitors are. By commenting on the posts of others in your network regularly, you'll get noticed more too.

If you'd like my free ebook called 30 Top Tips for Business Growth Using LinkedIn, please go to: www.smallbusinesshugesuccess.com/personalbranding

Twitter

Twitter is another place to shape your personal brand, because it's personal. People don't want to be talked at on Twitter, they want to interact. You can really engage with people on Twitter and develop relationships. As with all social media, you need a strategy for Twitter rather than simply signing up and telling everyone what you had for breakfast (unless you are a diet blogger, in which case you must tell everyone what you had for breakfast). Even if you'd rather tweet just for friends, remember it's public and so it still tells people about your personality and style.

Reasons to tweet:

- Start conversations with your current or potential customers, through which you'll gain valuable feedback and build trust.
- Offer rich content that builds your standing as an expert in your field.
- Learn about what people need.
- Learn about what others are doing and offering in your area.

Quick Twitter set up

Again pick a user name or 'handle' that is relevant and ideally your name.

Use the same avatar as for other social media profiles.

You may want a different cover photo, but still make sure it shows what you do and check the optimal size before you load so it doesn't get cut off or distorted.

Bios on Twitter are often a series of words that describe you to make the most of the short space.

Be yourself, follow who you want to follow and who is interesting to you, don't worry if people unfollow you, be consistent and don't be afraid to retweet important tweets such as your free ebook launch.

Be generous, retweet, comment and 'favourite' things you find cool or interesting or helpful.

My Twitter name is @AdeleMcLay. Check out my account and use it as a guide to creating your own. I'd be thrilled if you followed me on Twitter.

Instagram

Instagram is now rivalling Twitter as a platform of influence, especially for younger demographics (along with YouTube). With Instagram you have to be really clear about your personal brand style. One food photographer I know has set up a more personal Instagram account because her professional account is so clearly defined by her food shots that she doesn't want to put off her followers by uploading selfies! It takes dedication, but as a result her personal professional brand is incredibly strong and her audience are almost entirely raving fans who can't wait for her next workshop or book.

The fitness coach, Joe Wicks, has built an incredibly successful company on the back of his Instagram success. His personal style is instantly recognisable — a cheeky chap who throws ingredients into the pan for recipes that go alongside his programmes including Lean In 15. When combined with photographic before and after testimonials from people on the programme, it makes for a powerful and extremely popular brand that has produced record breaking book sales and many more partnerships in the pipeline.

I'm a big user of Instagram, as I see it as a very important platform. I currently have two accounts which you're welcome to follow: @AdeleMcLay and @Small.Business.Huge.Success

Pinterest

Pinterest is a great visual showcase for your style and taste. It is increasingly becoming a way to create a library of online content that you admire or find useful, as well as your own, like giving public access to your bookmarks. It can be great for telling stories, for example behind the scenes of your industry or how you put your products together (depending on what you can reveal!). It can also be very helpful when you are developing your own style, as you will be drawn to images and designs that may reflect your own values and audience. Think of it as a visual scrapbook. You don't have to make it public, but if you do then remember it's a part of your online presence.

My Pinterest account name is Adèle McLay. Given the work I do, at present it's not a big platform for me – that may change. Take a look at what I place on Pinterest. I hope it inspires you.

Facebook

Facebook can be tricky territory when it comes to your personal brand, but with the security and pages features available it needn't be a minefield. Many people do still combine their personal Facebook friends with their professional and just have one 'profile' on the network. From a long-term point of view, it's really a good idea to have a separate professional 'page', even if you'll have to invite some of your friends to like that page because you also work with them. However, even with your personal page settings set to 'friends only' there are still loopholes, if a friend decides to share your post for example. As with all things online, it pays to imagine your grandmother reading anything that you post before you go ahead!

Having a professional Facebook page is a useful place for colleagues and clients to connect with you, and also a link to any content you are publishing online. Some good examples include Guy Kawasaki and Adriana Huffington, who are admittedly rather well known but who do post great content. Try looking up people in your own network and see who is making the most of having a professional page. It's particularly good for people in the creative industries and professional services.

I have two professional Facebook pages, being AdeleMcLayFan and SmallBusinessHugeSuccess. I'd be thrilled if you joined my growing Facebook community on those pages. My personal Facebook account is strictly for family and close friends as I made the decision to use Facebook's professional business or fan pages for my work.

Snapchat

Snapchat, which is a type of visual messaging app where your posts only exist for a finite amount of time, is definitely the newish 'kid on the block' as I publish this book on personal branding. If your target audience demographic is younger, then it's likely that you'll have to embrace Snapchat as it's going from strength to strength as the next social media app. People are wanting to feel a part of a community and Snapchat offers that as 'stories' can be created and shared with your community, and live chats can be created.

Joined Up Social Media

The great thing with social media is how joined up you can be. You might post an image on Instagram that is a visual 'thought' or moment from your latest blog piece. So you can pop an invitation in your description to come over and read the full post. Then you can tweet the image and blog url with an intriguing line that will encourage people to click through. You can post the blog directly onto Google+ and your Facebook page or post the link, pin the image from the blog onto Pinterest and a week later post as an update on LinkedIn. Phew! Yes, this is just an example of what's possible, because if you're doing all this by yourself then you need to decide which platforms offer the best opportunities to connect and influence for you. Where do your customers or peers hang out, the people you want to be seen by? Join their conversations and gradually start your own with them. Ask for opinions, views and ideas, rather than only ever offering your own. And like every other aspect of personal branding, always be yourself.

Get Cracking and Build Your Platforms

The vast array of social media platforms can be so overwhelming that there is a temptation to either spread yourself too thin across them all or end up giving up because you're not seeing positive results fast enough. Go for the platforms that suit you and your customers or clients best — your community — and put your focus there until you create a snowball effect or tipping point. A hard working, well designed website needn't be complicated or expensive, and one of the best business networking sites in the world, LinkedIn, is free to join. So, choose your next online steps and set yourself some goals.

ACTION

Google your name. What do you need to improve your rankings?

_____

_____

_____

_____

Ensure you complete a full LinkedIn profile. What must you do to create a complete profile?

_____

_____

_____

_____

Create a personal professional website. What are the key elements you will include in your personal website?

_____

_____

_____

Which social media platforms are most suited to you and your audience (target the ones best suited to you)?

_____

_____

_____

Offline Platforms

'If opportunity doesn't knock, build a door.' – Milton Berle

There are a range of offline platforms that you can use to build and present your personal brand. Networking is a key platform that many business people use, and network events come in all forms. What about using the media and public relations to stand out? Would being quoted in a newspaper or magazine help your brand? Would being a commentator on TV or radio support you? All that can be achieved through the power of public relations. You could sponsor an event, advertise, or cold call to get noticed too. Then there's public speaking, perhaps giving keynote speeches, motivational speeches or an industry specific presentation.

Let's explore some of the many offline personal brand building opportunities that are available to you.

Networking

Sometimes a little self promotion is needed; it's not something to be embarrassed about. If you're running a business or trying to impress your potential employer, tooting your own horn in the right way to the right people can make a world of a difference.

So what is networking?

Networking is something you need to do if you want to expand your sphere of influence and therefore build your audience of people who will want to work with you, hire you or buy from you. It is not simply handing out business cards at endless networking events with no clear intention, statement or follow up in the hope people will contact you or read your blog. The most effective networking is positioning yourself as a valuable connection who others will want to share. When you think of networking, you need to think of it as a two-way dialogue that leads to a meaningful exchange. The golden rule is to remember it's not just about you.

Networking takes an investment of time, so it's important to be strategic with your networking activities and focus on the opportunities most likely to produce positive results and influential connections. You will need to give in order to most effectively connect, and so you need to give intelligently:

- Give to people who will immediately appreciate the value of what you are giving
- Give to people in ways that can be shared
- Give to people in ways that amplify your core brand message and offering
- Give with no expectation of return favours

If you are someone who struggles with saying 'no' to people and so often find yourself spread too thin, always helping out others without knowing why you're doing it, read this point again.

GIVE TO PEOPLE IN WAYS THAT AMPLIFY YOUR CORE BRAND MESSAGE AND OFFERING.

This is your filter. If you always say yes to every single request that means you're spending precious energy on things that have no relevance to your core brand, which means your brand will become diluted and lose impact. You may even find that when you do these 'off message' tasks or favours that they aren't even that well appreciated. So it's time to start filtering and only say yes to the people who really matter and to the things that will reflect what is at the heart of you and your brand: your strengths, skills and passions.

Remember in all the networking you do, when asked the question, 'what do you do?', it's a perfect time to use your elevator pitch. Be intriguing and great questions and conversations will follow.

My System for Networking Excellence

I'm an advanced networker, and it's a topic I'm often asked to talk about or touch on during keynote presentations and workshops I participate in. In my opinion, there are five key secrets of savvy networkers. They are:

1. Strategic Intent
2. Standing Out
3. Symbiotic Relationships
4. Sales Strategies
5. Systems and Automation

If you'd like to download my free ebook on the Five Secrets of Savvy Networking, please go to: www.smallbusinesshugesuccess.com/personalbranding to receive the ebook.

Networking is an important part of business and life, yet so many people lack the knowledge of how to do it effectively or feel intimidated by the thought of it. The key is to remember that networking is about building relationships and not trying to sell to the room or to the person you're talking to. After all, when you go networking, are you looking to buy something? I'm guessing not. Therefore, it's important that you don't try to sell your goods and services. Instead focus on getting to know people and connect with them again after the initial meeting and build the relationship. You never know where it might take you in business and life.

Networking Your Way to the Influencers

There will be times when you want to make contact with an industry influencer or potential future partner — people you're not already connected with. Perhaps you want to interview them or begin the process of building a relationship and then start talking to them about collaborating in some way. How do you make contact with these folks? Cold calling is generally not going to get you the results you want. Often direct emails won't either.

Cold calling was the way in which business was done, once upon a time. In the early years of my career, I did loads of cold calling very successfully, and perhaps I'm one of the few who actually like it. Times have moved on and seldom will your calls be answered when cold calling now. There are more effective ways to build relationships than cold calling, the simplest being to find someone who knows the person you want to meet and to ask for an introduction. LinkedIn can often help you as you can see who in your network is connected to the person you want to meet. You then ask that person to make an introduction. A word of warning though! Make sure you fully brief the person who is doing the introducing to ensure they know plenty of relevant information about you so that it is compelling for the person you want to meet to take your call or to want to meet with you too. If the introduction is not done effectively, then you'll struggle to get to meet that key person.

Networking mind map

Think of three influencers in your industry or area who you want to connect with and who are already connected with each other. Draw three circles in the centre of a blank piece of paper and put their names in the circles.

Now research people who are directly connected with those people and who are potentially closer to your own direct circle. See if you can find a path of connection between yourself and those top influencers.

How can you help?

Have a look at the people closest to you in your networking map and start to think of ways in which you can offer immediate value. What projects are they working on that you can help with in some way? Can you connect them to people, services or products? Ask them if they need any help right now. If it sounds like a lot of giving, it is, that's why doing what you love is so important as genuine giving is the best way to make long lasting connections with people. You can't fake it, or expect people to repay you, people can smell that a mile away. But the more amazing value you can offer, the more people will spread the word about you and your direct sphere of influence will expand.

Think about the ways in which you already tend to help people and how you can begin to offer that to others.

Here are some examples to help you create your own list:

- What do people always ask you?
- What have you learned from your own experiences that you can pass on?

Can you find ways to promote others whose work or products you love? This is a particularly effective strategy for people closer to your own network, rather than going straight to the top. Can you shine a light on people who are less known but who you really rate? When you learn something helpful from someone, go ahead and share that experience, linking to the person and letting them know.

When you buy people's products who are in your network and you find them really useful, be sure to post a review on your blog and/ or in your newsletter and let others know about your experience. Let the creator know about your experience. This can be a great way to create a connection with someone you don't know directly. Twitter is an amazing way to publicise your review and tag the person at the same time.

Join the conversation

One of the most powerful ways to amplify your personal brand and build your network is to join online and offline conversations that are relevant to what you do and what you stand for. These can include your passions as well as your work areas because one of the easiest ways to show your personality is through your interests, which will often be linked in some ways to what you do. For example a chef might talk about food and recipes but also join conversations about travel, photography or writing.

Top Tips for Networking Success

As you build your personal brand, you'll be doing more networking, so it's important you feel confident. Here are some top tips for networking success. You can also download my free ebook on the Five Secrets of Savvy Networking at: www.smallbusinesshugesuccess. com/personalbranding

If networking is new to you or if you feel uncomfortable networking and mingling, then I recommend the book, *How To Work A Room*® by my friend Susan RoAne. Her book is filled with strategies and tactics to support you to mingle and network in any business or life situation. Susan has been a coach, teacher and keynote speaker on this topic for over 25 years, and is second to none when it comes to the art of successfully making connections that matter and last, both in person and online.

Introduction strategies

The best way to find out if going to networking events is useful for building your personal brand and your connections is to try a couple out and make a plan ahead of time so that you give them your best shot. If there are people at the event who you would specifically like to meet then do some research to find conversation starters. You might even be able to introduce yourself by email or through LinkedIn before the event so that you'll be able to make an instant connection rather than making a cold approach. Make sure you have business cards to hand and feel confident with your elevator speech for the inevitable 'what do you do?' question.

Remember that people love to be given care and attention, so simply asking a question based on how they feel the event is going is an easy approach when speaking with an individual.

If you are introducing yourself to someone you wish to connect with, don't launch straight in with your specific agenda, but equally don't wait too long in the small talk zone so that you miss your opportunity to form that all important mutual bond. Asking questions that are relevant to the event are a great way to get started.

Approaching a group when networking

When you see a group of people busy with their conversations, all you need to do is try a simple 'May I join you?'. Once you're in the group, you need to be a participant, not a spectator. Be assertive, let them know you're there; ask questions that are open ended.

However, you don't want to appear brazen, just budging yourself in the group. If the group is already in a deep conversation about a particular topic, be sensitive. Wait for the appropriate time to enter the group and find a natural opening in the conversation.

The next step is just as crucial, it's knowing when to get out!

Make sure you have a follow up plan. Understand the why, if and how these people will be valuable to your network. Remember your main purpose; you're there for networking, not to glue yourself to one person or group.

Do the slip and slide

You and others like you are there for one purpose and one purpose only, to meet as many relevant people as you can, so you can add them to your network. However, there will come a point when you'll have to walk away. The best way to exit is to ask people for their business cards. That way you can end the conversation, leave and still have a connection to continue your conversation at a later date.

Here are a few examples of exiting strategies:

- 'If you will excuse me, I have to get going, but would you like to swap business cards so we can connect and continue this conversation?'
- 'Is there any way we can continue this conversation at some other time, I have a few ideas I'd like to discuss.'
- If you believe the conversation is leading nowhere and it's time to move on, try this, 'it was a real pleasure meeting you, but if you'll excuse me I see a friend I just need to say hello to.'

- Or your last resort, 'would please excuse me, I need to refresh my drink. Thank you for your time, it was a real pleasure. I hope to continue this discussion some other time over lunch or dinner. I hope you have a pleasant evening.'

Following up

What separates the networking giants from the dwarves is their ability to follow up. If you find yourself at an event, it's a good idea to jot down notes onto the business cards you've collected from various people, that way you know who's who, and what you learned from them.

24

No, it's not the television series, it's the time frame you need to follow up with your networkers. In the next 24 hours either make a call or send them an email.

- Deliver or ask for promised information.
- Show your interest about what was learned or said by repeating it in your follow up.
- Offer your services to the networker in return for their time.

Give, give, and give some more... then ask

So networking needn't be a dirty word if it's done for the right reasons. Forget about what other people can do for you, focus on what you can do for them. Give, give and give some more. You may be surprised at what comes back to you in ways you don't expect. Plus, if you've been a giver, if there ever comes a time and you genuinely need someone's help, it's more likely they will jump at the chance to reciprocate.

Can you create your own networking get together?

Jacqueline Burns was a publisher who went freelance to become an agent and ghostwriter. She realised she knew loads of people from the publishing world and that new writers could benefit a great deal from meeting them. Until your book is actually commissioned, publishing can feel like a closed-off industry that's almost impossible to find a way into, even just to talk to someone about how it works. What started as an informal gathering soon turned into the London Writers Club, a monthly gathering with a guest speaker from publishing, writing workshops and one-to-one coaching sessions. Jacqueline has taken on writers from the meetings and workshops to successfully represent their works to commercial publishers and also introduced authors to the ways in which it is now possible to self-publish. All from an initial desire to bring people together.

Media and Public Relations

Nowadays we don't need to employ marketing and PR agents to represent us. We can be our own PR guru, promoting ourselves and our expertise to media outlets to comment on issues relating to our subject.

Amanda Ruiz, my friend and PR expert who's known as 'The Ultimate Door Opener', believes that all business owners must know the art of self promotion, PR is simply the promotion of you and your expertise. Ruiz also says that journalists want to hear from you and not PR agents, so go for it, and be your own PR expert. Ruiz's seven secrets for getting your own press are:

Secret 1 – Find your 'golden nugget': what is the interesting information about you that you don't tend to tell people about as you know it so well? You must then decide your press angle. What do you want PR for? A product launch? Profile piece? New jobs in the area? A seasonal or local story?

Secret 2 – Research your ideal client, the competition and your target journalist:

Your client: What do they read online and offline? Where do they shop? What is their income? Hobbies? Use this information to create your own customer avatar and then use this information to identify the correct media to target.

Your competition: Where have they had press mentions, and what angles were used? This will inspire you to think of more potential angles.

Your target journalist: Read their articles, look them up on journalisted.com and LinkedIn, and follow them on Twitter. When you communicate with them, you will know their writing topics, and can mention their latest article to them which they'll appreciate.

Secret 3 – Prepare your PR Toolkit: this includes professional photographs, strong copy, and an up to date website with clear contact details.

Secret 4 – Your press release: it must be newsworthy – why do readers want to read about your business? Include a one-liner impactful headline, clear contact details, short sharp paragraphs, a quote, verifiable facts and relevant statistics if you have them.

Secret 5 – Your PR plan of action: you must be targeted. You will get the best results if you focus on your key targets and do quality follow ups as opposed to doing a mass mail out and hoping something will stick. So create a plan of action listing contact details, date of contact, feedback action to take.

Secret 6 – The PR campaign: start locally to practise your pitch before you go to the big guns. Never leave a voicemail as journalists are busy and you will want to call them again without appearing to be a stalker! Be persistent and always polite.

Secret 7 – Thank you: whenever you are featured, follow up with a thank you to the journalist. Then add the piece to your website and share it on social media.

And that's how you get your own PR. When you've achieved it once, set up a system and continue to repeat the process with each new PR piece you wish to promote. You can connect with Amanda Ruiz, PR expert for entrepreneurs and 'The Ultimate Door Opener', at www.amandaruiz.co.uk

Public Speaking

Many fear public speaking, in fact some fear it more than death! Yet public speaking is so important and can amplify your business success and life in so many ways. As my friend and speaking coach, Patricia Fripp says, 'Outside of the privacy of your own home all speaking is public speaking'. Public speaking is one of the most important skills you can develop in your life. It can have a major influence on your career and business success, and even the quality of your relationships.

When we think of public speaking, often we think of a stage with loads of people waiting to hear someone speak. Yes, that's public speaking. So is speaking and sharing your ideas with one, two or three others. So is giving a presentation to a group at a networking event, explaining what you do in your business. Public speaking takes many guises. It can also change the course of history. Think of Martin Luther King's, 'I Have a Dream' speech, or the speeches given by Nelson Mandela upon his release from prison and in uniting his country as President of South Africa.

Here are some key reasons why public speaking is an important platform for building your personal brand:

- You feel more confident in yourself and your topic when you are preparing and talking about it.
- You are able to verbally communicate your message and purpose in a way that helps people to get to know you, hopefully like and trust you, and that leads to them seeing you as an expert in your field.

- You can generate sales through public speaking. Some speakers learn how to 'sell from the stage' while speaking, whereas others share content only from the stage, and the sales follow afterwards if they have impressed their audience. The key is to understand how to effectively message your expertise so it resonates with your audience.

- The skills learned through public speaking can support the development of other skills including leadership and the ability to 'read' and understand others.

- One of the best ways to learn is to teach. Public speaking provides the opportunity to teach others and in doing so you must improve your own knowledge first during the preparation for the presentation.

- Most people avoid public speaking, so in being prepared and willing to speak, you stand out, you get noticed.

- You will grow your community through public speaking. As more people hear you teach your expertise, they will begin to connect with you, perhaps via your email community or on social media.

Remember, if you want to have a strong personal brand, you must be seen as a leader. Leaders must be able to communicate. Public speaking helps develop communication skills.

Advertising to Build Your Personal Brand

Advertising is still another relatively popular method for getting business, however its appeal is diminishing – think about how thin the Yellow Pages directories are these days. Often advertising is not the best method you can use to build your personal brand as it can be like taking a machine gun and spraying bullets, especially if you're not absolutely targeted with where you place your advertising. Some will hit the target but most others won't. Money will be wasted. To be effective, you must target the correct advertising medium – be a sniper – and make sure your target audience is fully represented where you are advertising. For instance, if you want to target chartered accountants with your advertising, then perhaps explore advertising with the professional bodies that represent chartered accountants as many have monthly magazines that are distributed to members, rather than (say) advertising in The Economist magazine.

The key is to have clarity about what you want to achieve through advertising, then to develop a strategy to support that goal.

Summary

These platforms that you are building are not only shop windows for your personal brand, but they also give you invaluable ways to interact with your audience, your potential customers or fans. Networking used to be a dirty word, it suggested old boys' clubs or a kind of nepotism or on the other hand had a whiff of desperation about it. But nowadays, networking has come into the 21st century and is so crucial for your personal brand, and in turn your business or career. Whether online or at a live event, these platforms put us in the same space as the people in our industry and the people interested in what it is we have to offer. Seth Godin suggests that one of the best ways to really stand out in your area is to either create an association, in other words organise your competitors and be the person in the room everyone knows, or start a school for what you do, a school for travel agents, a school for performance coaches, an apprentice academy. So, think creatively when it comes to platforms and networking. I know a couple of people who have spent 6 months crafting a TEDx talk, a long time to focus on just one platform, but it has led to hundreds of thousands of views, increased number of clients and book deals. Explore what is available to you and put your energy where it can really count.

ACTION

How can you integrate a networking strategy into developing your personal brand?

_____

_____

_____

_____

Can you benefit from being your own PR expert? How can you implement Amanda Ruiz's Seven Secrets for getting your own PR?

_____

_____

_____

_____

Where can you give presentations on your specialty topics to help build your personal brand?

_____

_____

_____

_____

Arianna Huffington

'Fearlessness is like a muscle. I know from my own life that the more I exercise it the more natural it becomes to not let my fears run me.'

Arianna Huffington launched The Huffington Post in 2005, one of the most widely read and linked-to global media brands on the Internet. She is the author of 15 books, most notably *Thrive: The Third Metric to Redefining Success* and *Creating a Life of Wellbeing, Wisdom, and Wonder,* and more recently, *The Sleep Revolution: Transforming Your Life One Night at a Time.* She has been included on the Forbes Most Powerful Women list and Time Magazine's list of the world's 100 most influential people.

Born in 1950 in Athens, Greece, Arianna Huffington moved to the UK when she was 16, later graduating from Cambridge, where she was president of the Cambridge Union debating society. In 1973, she wrote *The Female Woman*, an attack on the Women's Liberation movement and in particular Germaine Greer's *The Female Eunuch.* After moving to the US, she became a conservative commentator and was described by Margaret Talbot in The New Yorker as casting herself 'as a kind of Republican Spice Girl, a ditzy right-wing gal-about-town who is a guilty pleasure for people who know better'.

In 2004, she became a liberal, endorsing John Kerry in the presidential nominations. And so Arianna Huffington's personal brand reveals her willingness to evolve, which became the core stand-out aspect of The Huffington Post when it was launched a year later. The Huffington Post used the fact that it was digital rather than print to constantly test and be reactive to what readers wanted, testing headlines and moving popular stories, inviting bloggers to contribute (for free) and so becoming the go-to site for news, health, culture and comment. Even recently, Huffington introduced the 'What's Working' initiative, where the editorial team are encouraged to publish good news stories about people making a difference, 'positive contagion' as Huffington calls it, a departure from the usual news channels that concentrate on disasters and what's wrong with the world. It isn't only a desire to tell these stories, it makes perfect business sense as it opens up platforms like Facebook to the brand, where people tend to share inspirational stories rather than cold, hard news.

Back in 2007, Arianna Huffington was in her own words the definition of 'money and power' driven success. In her book *Thrive*, she describes fainting and cracking her head open from exhaustion just two years after launching The Huffington Post. It was her wake-up call, and became a time when she discovered her core values of well-being, wisdom, wonder, and giving that underpin her personal brand as it is developing today.

She redefined success as something that could be brought into alignment with what makes us happy, and she became freer with the spiritual side of herself that had always been there but often kept hidden.

Today, Arianna Huffington's personal brand is recognisable and distinct across all platforms. Her Twitter and Facebook head shots and banners are the same, featuring a nostalgic image of Huffington with her daughters when they were little girls. She talks openly of using tools like mindfulness and meditation and her feeds show a strong interest in mental health issues. She is still the girl-about-town of her youth, always stylish with a strong socialite streak, but also talks often about motherhood and that journey. And like many with such strong personal brands, she can be like Marmite, equally liked and disliked depending on whether she resonates. In addition to her bestselling book, she gives keynote speeches and has created the Third Metric conference, bringing together speakers and thinkers under the umbrella theme of redefining success in terms of those key values of well-being, wisdom, wonder and giving, using her vast network to collaborate with others to add power and strength to her cause.

The key lesson we can draw from Arianna Huffington is that it's ok to let your personal brand evolve as you do, so long as you try to maintain a sense of consistency across all the ways in which you communicate who you are as you evolve. Your brand, just like you, isn't set in stone, so you don't need to hold on to anything that no longer feels like a true reflection. If you need to refresh or tweak or even start over, do what feels right for you right now.

Chapter 7

Products

We live in a world that's focused on ideas, often big new and disruptive ideas. Who'd have thought that WhatsApp, Uber and Air B'n'B would be successful ideas and businesses? In developing your personal brand, whatever your industry, it's important you take your ideas and turn them into intellectual property (IP). The most successful people and businesses own IP in our fast moving world. IP is what will stand you apart from others in your niche.

As marketing expert, Seth Godin says: 'Finding new ways, more clever ways to interrupt people doesn't work. It's the person who knows how to create ideas that spread that wins today'.

We can turn our ideas and expertise into products that can be consumed in a range of ways by the community we're seeking to stand out in. Products are the new marketing tool. Creating our own solution frameworks are products and IP. They help us stand out. Create something useful and valuable and your customers and clients will do the marketing for you. They'll use social media to promote you – digital is the new marketing tool for us all.

Product creation also helps us to become more profitable in business. We take our community on a journey as we share our knowledge. If they trust and believe us to be an expert and the go-to person in our niche, eventually they will buy from us.

There are many types of products you may consider creating or curating that will help grow your personal brand, connect with your audience and give them even more reasons to like and trust what you do and what you stand for, that demonstrate that you're the go-to expert in your niche, and support your business to be more successful and profitable. A blog, a book or ebook, webinar or workshop, a tip sheet, a podcast, a new system for a way of doing things are all examples of products that you can create to position yourself as an expert in your niche.

For example, one of Seth Godin's key products is a daily blog. It's short, to the point and very honest about his thoughts on all manner of topics related to business and life.

The products that help position me as an expert in my field include writing a weekly blog, creating weekly YouTube videos on a range of topics related to business, life and personal growth, periodically hosting online summits, hosting a podcast where I interview business people, giving keynote presentations and motivational speeches, and of course, writing books.

As your brand develops, you may also develop products linked to you and your brand. For example, David Beckham has his football academies while Hemsley & Hemsley, healthy eating authors, have put their name to a spiralizer kitchen gadget after popularising courgetti in their cookbooks. Jamie Oliver is a master at creating products aligned with his personal brand, from restaurant chains to cookbooks, cookware, TV programmes, a foundation and YouTube channel.

These products are all the things that amplify your brand within your niche, they are part of the process of becoming irresistible, so you need to think carefully about what your niche needs and desires right now.

Think about someone like Robert Peston, who for a very long time was economics editor for the BBC before moving to ITV. Despite working for two large corporations, he has an incredibly strong personal brand not only through his recognisable style and tone but also 'products' including books, podcasts and radio programmes he has developed himself. He worked for one of the largest corporations in the UK while being completely true to himself, his personality, passions and strengths.

Perhaps you have been asked to put together presentations for clients or industry conferences; these are products. You might think of starting a blog related to your industry and begin to share your posts through LinkedIn Pulse. This is a fantastic way to share your ideas and build your reputation.

YouTube is the next wave of marketing. Think about it. How often do you Google or search YouTube for a 'How to'... or expert video? Many of us (me included) do it all the time. Have you thought about creating your own YouTube channel and uploading short to the point videos on your area of expertise? That's a product. Do that often enough with well thought out keyword search engine optimisation and I promise, you'll start to get noticed.

ACTION

Identify Potential Products

This exercise will help you identify a number of potential products that you could develop to enhance your personal brand and reputation, and offer your target audience something irresistible.

Write a list of 10 problems that your target audience share and often tell you about.

What is the solution *you* can offer to each of these problems?

What type of product would be best suited to each of your solutions? For example, a blog series, an ebook, video, webinar, workshop or system? It might be an information leaflet for new or potential customers, a side project at work to help address a specific problem or opportunity.

Problems	Solutions	Product creation ideas

Packaging your knowledge into products

- **Blogs**
- **Ebooks and books**
- **Webinars, YouTube videos**
- **Audio programmes/podcasts**
- **Membership**
- **Speeches (paid and unpaid)**
- **Workshops/seminars**
- **Online courses**
- **DVD programmes**
- **Coaching**
- **Certifications**
- **Masterminds**
- **Apps**

Blogs

Blogs are an excellent way of getting your personal brand noticed and building your credibility with prospective clients or current customers. Write the blog, put it onto your website or develop relationships with other bloggers and offer to provide a blog as a guest post. You can also repurpose your blog and place it on LinkedIn Pulse, another well recognised public blogging site.

Nowadays business people will often use the LinkedIn advanced search tool as their first port of call, so if you stand out and use industry specific keywords both in your profile and blog posts that you publish on LinkedIn Pulse, then you're going to be found far more quickly than others who have the bare minimum up on their LinkedIn profile. I know countless people (including me) who have been offered speaking engagements, business opportunities and collaborative projects through LinkedIn as a result of a fully completed profile and relevant blogs on the site.

The more specific or niche your subject can be, the better. Say, for example, you work in the catering industry and have a passion for finding incredible local ingredient inspired restaurants wherever you go on your travels – there are people who would love to read about how you find these places and then what you think of their recipes. Align that with being a locally sourced ingredient catering professional and you're creating content that is not only interesting and useful, it's adding credibility and depth to your personal brand, showing who you are and what you stand for.

Books and Ebooks

Writing a book or ebook is one of the most effective ways to build your personal brand and share your ideas or expertise with your audience. You may start with a short, free ebook that you encourage your readers to share freely. The great thing about creating a free ebook is that you can easily do it yourself, it's as simple as saving a word document as a pdf. However, as with any product you create, quality is essential because even if you are giving something away for free, it reflects your personal brand and how people rate you.

If you want to write and self-publish your own book that's specifically tailored to your industry then it can be a fantastic calling card that will add value to your personal brand. It does take an investment of both your time and finances so you need to be sure it's worth it; for example, if one new major client came on board with you as a result of the book and paid for the expenses it would be worth it! Or you might decide it's worth doing as a marketing expense to position you as a stand out expert in your field.

I know a person who owns a cleaning company in Scotland and he wrote a short book on house cleaning tips. He published it himself and gave it away to existing and potential customers. At the start of his entrepreneurial journey he only had a couple of cleaning staff to support him in business. Now he is licensing his brand to others because his business got so busy. That's the power of building a personal brand and using a book as a calling card. You get noticed. Not many other cleaning companies were doing that, so he stood head and shoulders above the others.

You might feel that your book idea is something that a publisher will want to commission, and there are many academics and business leaders who have enjoyed the personal brand boost of being published. If your idea suits a niche publisher then you'll be able to contact them directly, but if you think it has broad mainstream appeal then you'll need to get an agent on board who will represent you and your proposal to publishing editors on your behalf. (The best place to start to research the publishing industry is https://www.writersandartists.co.uk)

Podcasting

While the technology to support podcasting has been available since about 2006, it's really coming to the fore now. Hosting a podcast is not for everyone, but if it suits you and your industry and supports you to be seen as an expert in your field, then consider adding this as a product to enhance your personal brand, and ensure you have the podcast accessible from your website so it can easily be found by your community.

You can demonstrate your expertise and build your personal brand and podcasting community by creating your own content that you talk about during your podcast and/or you can interview or have conversations with others, which also amplifies your personal brand. A podcast is like a mini radio programme that you broadcast out to your community as often as it suits you. You can explore the different types of podcasts to get some ideas through apps such as Podbean, Castro and Overcast.

Webinars

Hosting webinars is another online tool you can use to build your personal brand and to demonstrate your expertise in your field. You invite your community to join you in a webinar which you host online. A webinar is like an online presentation with questions and answers at the end. You present your material and invite questions which you answer. Webinars are incredibly popular and can be used to share information or to sell products and services. Plus they can be automated, which means you can record the webinar once then offer it to your community enabling them to watch it at certain pre-determined times that you've specified or that suit them.

Giving Keynote/Expert Speeches

We've discussed the importance of being a speaker in chapter 6. Giving speeches is both a platform and product. You can give speeches for free to teach content to demonstrate your expertise, and as you get better known, you'll often be able to charge for your speeches. Some experts don't charge for their speeches, preferring to be able to sell their other products from the stage, for instance, books and courses. Speaking is an excellent product if you are prepared to master the craft.

Online Courses

Online courses are a very popular product to sell now as so many people want to undertake more learning online rather than reading books or attending workshops. The prices of online courses vary enormously from very inexpensive to vastly expensive. A word of warning, if you are buying online courses, make sure they are from reputable teachers, and if you are creating online courses yourself, make sure they are good quality and worth the money you are asking your customer to pay for them. The quickest way to tarnish your personal brand is to over-promise and under-deliver. Unsatisfied customers will certainly let you know about it too, and often their comments will be online and can go viral.

Create and Curate

Creating content from scratch takes a great deal of time and effort. It's worth it, though, because people will begin to recognise your content and your voice will strengthen. Your original content is your foundation, giving you masses of credibility. Build a library of what you write so that in time you can offer 'best of' articles. You might discover you have an ebook waiting to be published or used as an introductory offer. A series of videos might become the foundation of an online course.

You can also develop your writing skills by curating content. The Internet is crammed with so much content it's getting harder to navigate by ourselves and at the same time be sure of the quality. An excellent way to develop into a dependable author is to offer your niche audience curated content they can trust and feel confident about. For example, a life coach might offer a weekly in-depth book review of a self-help book, whether just published or a classic. A landscape gardener might do a weekly link to favourite gardens and explain the planting. A financial adviser might do a weekly round up of relevant articles in the news over the past seven days. Like your own original content, the key is to follow the same golden rules of quality, relevance, consistency (i.e. make sure you publish every week at the same time) and 'shareability'. Give people content that you'd love to be given yourself.

ACTION

Choose a product and begin to flesh it out. What do you need to do to create this product and how are you going to let people know about it? Be realistic about choosing a product that you can currently afford to see through to launch. If you need to learn new skills or make new connections to complete your product, such as learning how to create online videos or hiring someone who does, then get started right away.

_____

_____

_____

_____

_____

_____

Services into Products

If you're in the business of selling your knowledge as a coach, consultant, mentor, trainer or industry expert then I would hazard a guess that most often you are exchanging your time for money with your work, and that generally you must be present for this exchange to take place, i.e. that your work is 'one to one' or 'one to many' in a face to face environment. While many experts like to work this way, me included in my business and life strategy coaching and consulting work, there are other ways in which you can 'package' your knowledge into products, in addition to selling it as a service.

Think of the book *The Seven Habits of Highly Effective People* by the late Stephen R. Covey. Covey turned his knowledge into a system that become famous through his book and then trained consultants around the world to teach the seven habits to customers. Then there's Robert Kiyosaki's *Cash Flow Quadrant*. His cash flow system has taught millions of people around the world. Sam Horn is a world renowned consultant and author of 13 books. She coaches people to stand out when pitching, presenting, promoting or persuading decision makers in any situation. Her INTRIGUE system has been turned into a book called *Got Your Attention*, and a TedX Talk, and Horn uses her INTRIGUE system when working with clients whether it be one on one or in groups, workshops or in keynote speeches.

What these and many other experts have done is to distil their knowledge into a teachable framework. The framework helps the expert teach their material to others, and it also helps customers more easily learn the material. This is what it means to turn your knowledge into products and anyone selling services can package their services into bespoke products.

Creating a Framework

A product framework identifies the current problem, the desired outcome of the problem and the route to achieve the outcome. The framework is a bit like a road map. If you are in Texas and you want to drive to New York, it's best to follow a roadmap to achieve your goal, as if you don't know the roads, you may end up somewhere unexpected and unintended. It's the same with knowledge sharing. If your customer has a problem, they need a system or route to solve it.

Frameworks are created in a range of ways. It could be a model, blueprint, system, template, matrix or method. To stand out in your market, it's important that you create your own framework rather than using one from another expert, otherwise they will get the credit and you're merely the consultant who delivered the material.

Take my Personal Branding Star System™ for example. That's my own trademarked system for guiding you in creating your own personal brand. By creating your own system you are elevating your expert status in the market.

Once you have created your framework, you can then decide how you productise it. You may give some of it away as free content in blogs, videos or webinars. You could also write a book about it (just as I am doing here). You may run workshops or seminars, sell online courses, give keynote speeches, create mastermind groups and coach clients one on one. The product creation possibilities are considerable as are the prices that you can charge. As a customer goes through your customer product journey with you, they will pay more for what you're offering as it gets more exclusive.

A Customer's Journey with You

My aim in this book is to have you build your personal brand so that you grow your business. I want you to stand head and shoulders above your competition. I want you to be the one people think of when they need a product or service you sell.

Depending on what you do, you may have a range of products or services you offer to your customers. There may be a range of price points too. If a customer is new to you and your business and they don't know much about you, they may want to get to know you first and experience your free content or your inexpensive products and services before spending heavily with your business.

Let's take a women's beauty salon. If a new customer walks through the door, they may ask for a simple manicure the first time they use the salon. If the beauty consultant does a good job, is personable, and demonstrates that they know what they're doing, the customer may return to purchase other, more expensive products and services at a later date. What if the salon invited the customer to join their emailing list where periodically (perhaps weekly or monthly) the salon emailed beauty tips, and perhaps had a YouTube channel where they videoed tips and ideas for women? Do you think the customer and potential customers would be impressed (if the consultant(s) do a good job at demonstrating and teaching their skills)? I think so. The chances are higher that they'll get new and repeat business. They can also make offers of other services and products, all packaged in bespoke ways, perhaps with interesting and alluring names to entice the customer. The salon may also be selling third party physical products too – nail polishes, make-up, hair products, which they can promote to their customers. If the salon continues to demonstrate their expertise, and are seen as the go-to salon for women, then they'll reap the benefits of increased and more profitable business.

This is the power of taking your existing and potential customers on a journey with you. They get to know and trust you. All business owners can create a customer journey with their community in order to build their personal brand and to demonstrate expertise, whether you're a dentist, specialist doctor, interior designer, electrician, architect, web designer or any other business in the market. Do it well, and your personal brand will be augmented and that will lead to increased sales.

What about a business coach? If their top package is one on one coaching, until they build credibility with their potential customer, they are unlikely to win many clients. But if they have that potential customer in their community and are regularly blogging or creating videos with good content, perhaps presenting free webinars about their own business success framework they've created, writing books, or offering low cost workshops, the potential customer will get to know the business coach, and will decide how good they are and if they resonate with that person. If so, the customer may purchase one on one coaching.

The journey can be a lot of free content and then paid products and services. It can be free, then low cost products, middle priced products and then high end products. It really is dependent on what your business is, and how your business model is created. We discuss this more in chapter 9 on Profitability.

Summary

In this chapter I have outlined some of the possible ways that products can help to enhance your personal brand. These are the products that help you stand out from the crowd, get recommended or have customers coming back and, when the time is right, spending more. If you sell actual products, then even these will reflect your personal brand to a degree if you own your business. They reflect your taste and expertise, for example. And if you can create added value products, like a tip series, a webinar or ways in which the customer can best use your service or products, you will soon stand out as the person who goes the extra mile, who is generous and really cares about them. That's when someone goes from being your customer or client into being a fan who won't hesitate to recommend you.

ACTION

What is the journey potential customers take with you and your business? Think about a potential customer hearing about your business and joining your mailing list. What products could you create that takes them on a journey with you, where you and your business showcase your expertise?

_____

_____

_____

_____

_____

The 14th Dalai Lama

'Compassion is the radicalism of our time.'

With his red robes and smile, the 14th Dalai Lama, born Tenzin Gyatso, has become a symbol of compassion throughout the world since fleeing his native Tibet in 1959. He has written many books, perhaps most notably *The Art of Happiness,* and has travelled the globe teaching and speaking and spreading a message of love and kindness. In 1989, he was awarded the Nobel Peace Prize.

Dalai Lamas are important monks of the Gelug of Yellow Hat school of Tibetan Buddhism. Each Dalai Lama is considered to be the next in a line of tulkas believed to be incarnations of the Bodhisattva of Compassion. 'Dalai' means ocean and 'Lama' means guru.

Like all our case studies, there are immediately recognisable aspects to him that make him stand out. The robes are obvious but essential, depicting a holy man, but his individuality goes beyond the robes. When people picture the Dalai Lama's face it will most often be smiling or laughing. His words and messages are not over-complicated, he transmits a hope for peace and for people to simply be kinder to each other in his very being. Many people across the globe look to him for specific guidance and teachings, as people of the Catholic faith look to the Pope. As an individual, he has an incredible amount of responsibility on his shoulders, and yet has a way of not letting the weight of the world push down on him. Just as the Buddhist teachings encourage, there is always a feeling of 'flow' around him. There is a lightness in his being.

It is not simply his position though that makes the Dalai Lama so recognisable and such a potent brand. His character comes through in every speech or talk or teaching, his ability to connect with people and therefore create love and loyalty, to encourage many others to pass on the Buddhist messages of compassion for all beings.

And he has even embraced the modern communication platforms, with 12 million likes on Facebook and another 12 million followers on Twitter. There is an official website with teachings as well as news and events. There you can read His Holiness's 'commitments' or values, which are to promote the values of humanity such as tolerance, forgiveness and contentment, to promote harmony among all religions and to preserve Tibetan Buddhist culture. These values provide a core foundation to everything he says and does.

In this way, the Dalai Lama provides us with an excellent example of how products may enhance and expand your personal brand. The books, for example, give people from so many different backgrounds the chance to understand his teachings without having to go to see the man in person, the opportunities to do that being few and far between for the vast majority.

As the Dalai Lama himself says, 'the institution of the role will only exist so long as enough people want it to exist. As soon as it is no longer relevant it will cease to exist. I'm not worried about that.'

Chapter 8

Partnerships

> 'Coming together is a beginning, keeping together is progress, working together is success.' – Henry Ford

Teaming up with the right people for the right reasons is a key way to build the awareness of your personal brand and your business. You need to be careful to ensure shared common values and create collaborations that are mutually beneficial and offer the customer or end user something really special. Do that and you'll leap up the ladder of success.

There are two key questions to ask when you are thinking about potential collaborations:

1. What is it that I want to achieve?
2. How do I best get there?

If you realise that it's going to be easier getting to where you want to be by teaming up with others in some way then you can start thinking about the best way to go about it. Don't jump into collaborations just for the sake of it, or because someone else asked. Be open and receptive but also scan these opportunities through your personal brand filter to make sure they don't pull you off at a tangent or dilute your brand. The thing about collaborations is that when they're right they can help us take significant leaps towards our goals, but when they're wrong they can hold us back and cause a frustrating delay.

The brand Small Business Huge Success™ was founded by me, and is collaborative. The purpose of the business and brand is to inform, inspire and impact small business owners and entrepreneurs around the world who want to achieve the business success and personal freedom they dream of. It's really important that I find the right partners in this work, people who connect with the vision I have for the business and share my personal and business values. In finding likeminded people, the chances are higher that we will work together successfully for the benefit of the global community we serve through the brand.

The development of successful partnerships takes time. All parties must want to support the others to be successful. Be clear about what you want to achieve in developing partnership arrangements. As my friend and joint venture expert, Helen VandenBerghe says, 'When creating joint ventures think about the long term. Rather than inviting someone to partner just on one specific project, discover what their goals are for the next year or two, and build a proposal that gives you both multiple opportunities to support each other and helps them achieve their goals'.

Types of Partnerships

Partnerships come in all forms: sales (often by way of referral partners and affiliate relationships), content co-creation and investors are three of the main types. Think carefully about your reasons for developing partnerships, and then set about finding the right partners for your business.

Referral Marketing

As you build your personal brand, the loyalty of your audience increases, as does your credibility and influence. Others may come to you and ask if you would be interested in referring their products or services to your audience, or vice versa that they would like to refer you to theirs. This is called 'referral marketing' and is based on trust and recommendation, and is designed to be mutually beneficial. For example, a nutritionist may build up strong reputation over time through their blog and media presence. They might have a local gym that they always go to and gradually a relationship forms based on mutual interest and respect. The gym might therefore ask the nutritionist if they would like to become the recommended nutritionist associated with that gym for any members who were keen to change their diet as well as improve their fitness. And in return the gym would have a great 'extra' service as part of their offering, helping them to stand out from the competition and show great customer service (retaining members is a constant challenge in the gym industry). There might not even be any financial exchange, but as a collaboration it works for all involved, the customers, the gym and the nutritionist.

Referral marketing works really well with property trades too. A builder will have a preferred roofer, electrician, plumber, kitchen designer and installer, painter/decorator, perhaps even landscape gardener, interior designer and architect that they work with and refer business to. If all those businesses get to know each other, and consistently do great work, then they will all continue to pass referrals to each other. It's a win/win relationship for everyone.

Affiliate Marketing

An affiliate partnership is where one party promotes the products and services of another for a commission. This happens in many situations in business and has become more prolific with people who are marketing their businesses online.

A real estate agent may sell a property and recommend the buyer to their preferred mortgage broker to arrange the finance. If a deal is done between the buyer and mortgage broker, the broker will pay the real estate agent a fee. This is pretty common practice in that industry, often called paying finders fees.

Perhaps you've developed your own framework to solve a customer problem. You may meet someone who has a community or email list who is happy to promote your framework and solution to their community for a percentage of the sales revenue. The beauty of this arrangement is that you and your system get promoted to a new community by someone they respect, so you'll likely get kudos on the back of the marketing. If members of that community 'opt-in' to your email list to receive free content, then you're growing your list too. If they buy your products and services, then you'll make money, although you'll be sharing a fairly large percentage of the revenue with your affiliate partner.

There are very good automated systems available in the market that enable online marketers to effectively develop multiple affiliate partnerships and to keep track of opt-ins and sales.

Content Co-Creation Partnerships

As the saying goes, 'two heads are better than one'. At times there are opportunities to co-create information or products that better serve a community using the relative skills of the experts. This can happen in any industry.

In the expert or coaching industry, it's not uncommon for experts to come together via online summits, webinars or in workshops where they co-create a product. For instance, I created and hosted the Business Networking Online Summit in April 2016 as one of the services offered by Small Business Huge Success™ where I interviewed 42 of the world's leading experts on topics tightly or loosely connected with business networking. With me interviewing these experts, we created a fabulously successful summit for all the participants so they could improve their own skills in business networking.

Giving and Collaborating

Can you think of opportunities already at your fingertips for collaborating with peers or colleagues that will collectively build your personal brand? For example, creative collectives are popping up all over the place providing a menu of services from which clients can pick according to their needs.

Here's an exercise to help you quickly identify potential collaborations:

Write down all the people in your immediate network whom you could add value to. What are the things you know about that might be of help? Could you simply start by promoting what they are great at to your audience?

Name	How I can add value

As you begin to promote and help others, then connections will form and potential points of collaboration will appear.

Interviewing Other Experts and Being Interviewed

Interviewing other experts through a podcast or webinar is a great way to get started with collaboration. It's amazing the knock-on effect this has for bringing up further opportunities. If an interview or webinar sounds too daunting then start with written blog interviews. Also, think about how your expertise in one field might be of real help to people who are connected to your industry but are either in a different role or aren't on the inside. For example, if you are a digital marketer, you might offer publishers the opportunity to give free talks to their authors on how to develop their online presence. The publisher gets to offer something really useful to their authors (tick author care and book sales) while you increase your profile and credibility and might even meet a few potential clients.

Now make a list of people you could interview and why:

Name	Interview Topic

Summary

Partnerships are one of the most effective ways to amplify your personal brand. When we combine our skills with those of others then if we get the recipe right the sum will be greater than the individual parts. If you have an amazing service that someone you genuinely admire and respect wants to recommend through their website or newsletter, that's a simple and effective collaboration. If you have a fantastic book idea but you don't have the time or skill to write and structure the whole thing, you just need to partner up with someone who can listen and get your voice and ideas down into words on the page. If you can come together with others to put together a stand out conference for your industry or an association or networking evening, go for it. Never be afraid to collaborate, just always remember to go back to your values and make sure they are aligned with any potential partnerships.

ACTION

Think of a project you are passionate about but haven't managed to progress to where you want it to be.

How could someone you know help move it forward?

_____
_____
_____
_____
_____
_____
_____

Can you put together a plan of collaboration?

_____
_____
_____
_____
_____
_____
_____

Meryl Streep

'For me, acting is total immersion into possibility.'

With 18 Academy Award nominations and three Academy Awards for Kramer vs. Kramer, Sophie's Choice and The Iron Lady, Meryl Streep is considered one of the greatest actors in a generation. Her ability to completely transform herself into the character she is playing is her gift and her craft. She is one of a few women who continue to be given great roles when many are thwarted by a sexist Hollywood industry when they no longer look young or pretty enough, as she put it herself, 'working our butts off to put women's stories on the screen'.

Meryl Streep's talent is to immerse herself in a character, but she says she has always shied away from giving acting advice to others because for her it isn't a method, it's a feeling deep down in her, it's a trust in herself and a deep belief in the character. She does what she does because she loves it, 'my heart starts to race when I read a character I want to do'. She finds acting infinitely interesting, and that is the key to why audiences will seek out her performances, from the harrowing Sophie's Choice to the hilarious Devil Wears Prada and Julia & Julia.

When asked in an interview how she would like to be remembered, Streep answered, 'with love by my family'. Streep's private life is private and her family is the most important thing to her, which adds even more credibility to her personal brand. She isn't on Twitter, there is no Instagram feed. This isn't to say those things aren't an important part of many personal brands, but for Streep it just isn't who she is and wouldn't sit right, and it's an important lesson to take the time to find what is right for you. After all, she is one of the most successful, loved and respected actors in the present day because she focuses all her work energy on the work itself. She described acting to be 'at its best like flying', or 'like a piece of music'.

One of Streep's characteristics is to believe in her capabilities, a trait nurtured by her mother, while understanding her limitations, 'I have a pretty good idea of what I am not good at, and have it front and centre of my consciousness every minute I am doing it'. This gives her a grounded strength and composure, she know she isn't a fraud, but someone who is doing what she can to the best of her abilities. She is also strong enough to say what she thinks, not what she thinks others want to hear from her. When asked if she was a feminist she replied, 'I am a humanist'. She went on to say that she believed gender inequality to be as much a man's issue as for women, and that for there to be change, men needed to feel odd when sitting around a boardroom table with few or no women in the room. She has also said that the world needs more of the traditionally feminine values such as grace, respect, reserve and empathy, values that infuse her own work and person.

Streep is a wonderful example of doing what makes your heart really sing and then working really hard at it. In a world of distractions that has captured so many 'celebrities', she continues to do what she can as best she can, telling the stories that make her heart race and that allow her to fly.

Chapter 9

Profitability

'If people like you they will listen to you but if they trust you then they will do business with you.' – Zig Ziglar

So, now you know all the key tools for building your authentic personal brand, and all the previous pillars of personal branding success lead up to this point, where you get to turn all that hard work into profit. You might be really well known and admired in your field because you have taken the time to align your values and passions with what you do, you might present yourself well and be memorable at events and you are on your way to developing a social media strategy that is bringing you into the conversation with some of the major influencers in your industry.

And yet, this is often where it feels like there is a gap between the effort you are putting in, the quality you are delivering and the rewards you are reaping. In other words, the value that is being placed on your efforts and delivery isn't as great as it should be.

It's time to look at your business model in relation to your personal brand and ensure you are maximising the opportunities you now have to increase your profitability.

Your Business Model

This book is about building your personal brand and using it to become more successful in business, and to sell more of your products and services; in other words to create a more profitable business.

Therefore, there needs to be a clear return on investment connected to building your personal brand. You will be spending a lot of time and effort in building your personal brand, so we must make sure it's correctly monetised too.

The monetisation of your personal brand in business will be different for everyone. Some will be selling themselves as coaches, consultants, speakers, trainers, authors whereas others will be selling products and services through big and small businesses.

To build a successful business through the power of your personal brand, it's really important to have consistency between your personal brand and delivery of your business model to the market you serve. It's about being focused on and achieving business excellence too. What's the point of building a superb personal brand and having a string of eager potential customers knocking on your door, only to be let down because you and/or your business didn't deliver on your personal brand message (and possibly your business brand's customer promise)?

Business Excellence means having clarity and direction in each of these key areas of your business:

- Strategy
- Branding
- Marketing
- Sales
- Finance

- Team
- Customer
- Leadership

Here's a visual depiction of my Model of Business Excellence.

You can see that strategy is at the heart of all the other levers of your business and that leadership surrounds it all. Let's look briefly at each of the elements of the Model of Business Excellence.

Strategy

Business strategy comprises vision, purpose, values (culture), value proposition(s), market, company promise, key activities and key performance indicators or KPIs.

You're probably thinking, 'well I've done a lot of that work in Passion and Positioning', and in many respects you are correct. If you're a one-person business or a solopreneur, where you are selling yourself and your products and services, then yes you've done the work. The personal branding pillars of Passion and Positioning are the key elements of your strategy.

If you are a bigger business, perhaps with several owners, multiple divisions and staff, then your personal brand strategy may be slightly different to the business strategy. Your personal brand strategy will be interlinked with the business's strategy.

Branding

Branding comprises the business's branding as well as your personal branding. We've done much of the work on your personal brand; often it's important that your business is branded too. If you are your business, a one person business or solopreneur, then maybe you don't need to worry about your business brand as people will mostly remember and seek out you as opposed to being concerned about the name of your business.

If you are in a bigger business, or your business is strongly branded (regardless of its size) then company branding is important and should be actively created and managed. Remember, if there are number of owners or partners in the business, then they will all be slightly differently personally branded according to who they are and what they do in the business, but there should be alignment and harmony with the business's and their individual personal brands.

Marketing

Marketing in a business comprises channels, communications, capturing leads, and return on investment or ROI. We've already considered some of these elements in relation to your personal brand.

A channel is another name for platforms. What are your channels to market as a business? What is the style of communication your business uses to communicate what your business does to your target audience? Is there consistency in style between what and how the business communicates and how you communicate via your personal brand?

Modern businesses capture leads through some type of automated system. This is very important. What systems do you have in place for lead capturing and how will your business continue to message its expertise to your customers and email community who are potential customers?

What is the ROI on your marketing and personal branding time and expenditure? Effective businesses are measuring, monitoring and evolving this activity at all times, regardless of the business's size.

Sales

Sales, we all need them to thrive in our business, yet this is an area that so many business people struggle with. Whereas marketing communicates your messages within your desired channels, captures leads, nurtures potential customers through your marketing funnel, sales is about making a sale and having the money arrive in the bank.

To be effective in sales, you must have a sales strategy; you must execute your strategy with precision in order to make the sales, and you must continually review what you're doing.

If you are a solopreneur, then most often the marketing and sales process is dependent on you, although you may have some contracted support. Your selling strategies, style and technique must be consistent with your personal brand, so be sure you get coaching on effective selling if this is not a natural or practised skill for you. If you are a bigger business, perhaps you have a sales team, or call centre or both. All businesses are different. Your sales processes must work seamlessly with marketing and must be congruent with your personal brand and business growth aspirations.

Team

Your team is a critical component of your business. In the most successful businesses, teams live and breathe the business's values in support of owners. In modern businesses, teams are often made up of full-time, part-time and outsourced people. For your business to thrive you must focus on the recruitment, engagement, performance and retention of your team members. The long term success of your business depends on having the 'right' team members in your business. Get it wrong, and it can be costly in many ways including lack of engagement and that can also impact your personal brand. On many occasions, I've built relationships with people who have strong personal brands and values, only to be let down due to the customer experience from staff, as their mode of operation and perhaps personal values weren't congruent with that of the owners. This is not good for the business and damages all the work you put into building your personal brand in support of your business.

Customers

You are in business to serve the customers in your market niche. They are your *raison d'etre*. Without customers you don't have a business. Therefore your business model must always be considering your market niche. How do you deepen the relationships with your customers? What products and services are you offering now? What do your customers need going forward? How do you deliver your products and services to your customers? Operationally can you be more effective and efficient in how you serve your customers? What about innovation? How can you better serve your customers?

These issues are critically important in business, and if you demonstrate that you're listening to your customers, they will 'get' that you care and want to deliver more value to them. Your personal brand and reputation will be augmented in doing this.

Finance

For some business owners, the thought of understanding the finances turns them cold. Yet, this is a critically important area of business. Too many business owners allow the 'tail to wag the dog', meaning they don't understand or control the financials in their businesses. Is this linked to personal branding? Yes. What a waste of time building your personal brand in your business is if you haven't got a sustainable and profitable business. You must understand the numbers and manage the financial side of the business professionally.

Leadership

Leadership surrounds all the elements of the model of business excellence. As a business owner you must embody the idea of being a leader, even if it's only of yourself in the early days of building your business. As you build and grow your business, your team will rely on you to be a leader.

Leadership is about the 5Es. Envision. Enroll. Embody. Empower. Evaluate. As a leader you envision the future; you enroll others in support of your vision; you live and breathe the purpose, vision, values of the business so you are seen to be totally congruent with them and as a result you're seen as real and trustworthy. Your team will be magnetised towards you, as will customers. You empower your teams within their areas of work, and you continually evaluate – you look for ways to better serve. All of this is you living your personal brand. Do this well, and your business will thrive.

Summary

As you develop your personal brand over time, new opportunities will present themselves and it will be up to you to turn these into increased profits for you and your business. It is often difficult for people who are solopreneurs, freelancers or those who run their own business to be both the inspirational heart of the business and at the same time know what their work, products or services are truly worth. You might feel you need some professional advice or guidance in one of the areas of business excellence I have included in my model, and in the first instance when opportunities do come knocking as a result of your growing personal brand presence, simply start to ask yourself some key questions about how much effort they will require for the potential rewards.

ACTION

Review the Model of Business Excellence in relation to your business. How do you stack up? Is there congruence between the messaging you're displaying in building your personal brand and what's happening within your business? If not, what needs to change?

Strategy

_____

_____

_____

Branding

_____

_____

_____

Marketing

_____

_____

Sales

_____

_____

Finance

_____

_____

Team

_____

_____

Customer

_____

_____

Leadership

_____

_____

_____

Steve Jobs

Entrepreneur Profile

'Here's to the crazy ones, the misfits, the rebels, the troublemakers, the round pegs in the square holes.'

As a natural born innovator, Steve Jobs didn't sell computers, he sold 'tools to unleash your creativity'. He introduced the MacBook Air as the 'world's thinnest notebook' and the iPod as '1000 songs in your pocket'. He knew that brands weren't about 'things' but were about helping customers to fulfil their own dreams and needs.

Steve Jobs was considered one of the best presenters in the corporate world, and his TED talk 'How to live before you die' (watched more than eight million times) took his personal brand beyond corporate life to become an inspiration to so many before he died of pancreatic cancer. His message to others was consistent and powerful, to listen to your inner voice and follow your own path, to find out what you really care about and what drives you.

'The ones who are crazy enough to think they can change the world, are the ones who do.'

Jobs was born in San Francisco, California, in early 1955. He was born to two University of Wisconsin graduate students who gave him up for adoption. He grew up in Mountain View, California, which later became known as part of 'Silicon Valley'. He struggled with school as his mind easily became bored with regular classes, but he loved to work on electronics in the family garage with his father. He went to college, but dropped out after just six months; he did however continue to drop in on a few creative classes, including calligraphy, the seed of his passion for typography.

In 1974, Jobs briefly became a video game designer at Atari before travelling to India, where he began to understand the power of intuition and where he was introduced to Zen Buddhism. After returning to Atari, Jobs reconnected with Steve Wozniak, whom he had met while at high school and Wozniak was at college. In 1976, they started up Apple Computers out of Jobs's garage. By 1980 the company became a publicly traded company worth an estimated $1.2 billion at the end of the first day of trading.

Jobs was phased out of the company during the 80s but later returned as CEO in the 90s, and under his leadership Apple ranked at #1 on Fortune Magazine's list of 'America's most admired companies' and #1 among Fortune 500 companies for returns to shareholders.

He died in 2011 from pancreatic cancer, leaving a legacy to the company that went beyond innovation and technical excellence. In his own words, he created a company that didn't just make computers, but was 'technology married with liberal arts, married with the humanities, that yields us the results that make our heart sing'. Jobs pursued perfection, he worked and worked to create simplicity and opportunity for the consumer. His own personal style reflected the Apple style; understated, minimalist and creative. He was more of an architect than an engineer, he was a visionary who shows us what is possible when you have a great passion for life and what you do with it. His true passion was to create tools that people would use to add value to the world. He made it happen.

'Do what you believe is great work. And the only way to do great work is to love what you do. If you haven't found it yet, keep looking. Don't settle.'

Chapter 10

Performance

> 'The man who starts out going nowhere, generally gets there.'
> – Dale Carnegie

I coined the phrase: Dream It. Believe It. Work It. Achieve It. The dream is the easy bit. The hard work, sweat and tears come with believing in yourself and doing the work. Often at the start of a journey we have great belief, then we suffer knockbacks and our confidence is shattered. Both are normal. Success isn't linear — there will be many twists and turns, bumps and bruises coming your way in life and business as you work towards achieving all that you desire.

For all of my adult life I've been studying high performing people, working out what makes them achieve as they do in business and often (although not always) in life. I've intensely studied psychology, spirituality and personal development for more than 30 years, initially as a young university graduate, then banker, business adviser and strategist, entrepreneur, business growth coach and life strategist, investor. I'm fuelled and inspired by the answers I find in the stories of others, whether they're my clients, friends, strangers I meet, or people I hear of or read and watch videos about.

I've come to realise that people who achieve the goals they set themselves are just like you and me. The only difference is that they think more strategically and take massive action to put those strategies into practice. Fortunately, their habits and skills can be acquired.

You've got the tools to build your personal brand that when implemented will support you to achieve more success. The seven pillars of my Personal Brand Star System™ being: Passion, Positioning, Personalisation, Platforms, Products, Partnerships and Profitability will show you the way. So are you ready to get on and do the work? I truly hope so. That's the +1 pillar in my system – Performance.

Seven Strategies of Performance

There are seven key strategies that you must focus on to achieve what you want in business and life. They are:

1. Clarity
2. Vitality
3. Focus
4. Mindset
5. Excellence
6. Relationships
7. Self-expression

Approach the strategies with an open mind, a dash of curiosity and a spirit of adventure and they will reward you. Let's explore them.

Clarity

We need a very clear picture of what we are trying to achieve. I call it *seductive clarity*. If the picture we have is so seductive, when the going gets tough, which it will, we will still work towards achieving all we desire because it matters to us. Successful people have a clear purpose and inspiring vision and supporting goals that set them on a path to success, as they define it.

Vitality

This may make you feel a bit edgy, but *soulful vitality* is important. We need mental, physical, and psychic energy to be living and working at our best. Increasingly, successful people are looking after all aspects of their physical, emotional and spiritual health. That means nurturing our bodies and minds, choosing joy, and practising gratitude and generosity.

Focus

Performance is about *steadfast focus*. We need meticulous action in place to take us from where we are now to where we want to be. Successful people always have a plan. They seldom get distracted or if they do, it's not for long, because they've learnt how to focus on what's important. They do the work. When you treat focus as a skill you can develop, you find your productivity goes up, but the effort doesn't overwhelm you.

Mindset

Successful people cultivate a positive, optimistic and proactive mindset. They face down their fears, zap negative self-beliefs and discard those habits that do not serve them. They feel calm about potential problems and confident that they can tackle them. They have the mental resources to build a blueprint for success. In short they have a *sensational mindset*.

Excellence

I believe we should do and be the best we possibly can. Successful people settle for *skilful excellence* not perfection. They get on and do things. They try out things. They know the importance of lifelong learning and exceeding their own expectations of what they can do. They embrace change, fail forward and give and receive feedback that takes them to the next level of skill.

Relationships

We need our relationships to be at the heart of everything we do. Successful people know that their achievements are possible because they are part of a team at home, at work and in their community. They build professional networks that assist and inspire them to reach their goals. They work on creating more joy in their friendships and relationships with family. They build links with their community and they lead and inspire others. When we have what I call *sincere relationships* with others we open ourselves up to connections we could never have imagined.

Self-expression

We need to explore our authentic self, and develop and use it. For me it's about *stupendous self-expression*. Successful people know who they are and what's important to them. They have breadth in their lives; interests, passions, hobbies, adventure. Self-expression leads to developing curiosity about the world, communicating more clearly, experimenting with creativity, and exploring your adventurous self. Self-expression makes us feel good and whole. It adds a *'je ne sais quoi'* element to life.

What's This Got To Do With Personal Branding?

Everything! Get the seven key strategies of performance working in your life, and you'll find you'll be more fired up, and more inspired and motivated to achieve all that you desire. Your personal brand will come alive with your energy and enthusiasm. As more people recognise you as a branded person, you'll be more excited to continue on with the journey of doing the work of building your personal brand.

Performance is about doing the work that's required to make your dreams come true, remembering the seven key success strategies. Let's explore several of the key strategies to success in a bit more detail.

You Need Seductive Clarity

The only way to create the success you want in business is by conjuring a vision so compelling that you're fired up to choose, day after day, the belief and behaviours that will take you all the way to fulfilling it. Without an irresistible sense of what you want, you're not going to make it.

In relation to the development of your personal brand, you've done this work in the Passion pillar of the 7 +1Ps. You should have clarity about your heart of passion, purpose, vision and values.

Look After Yourself

Soulful vitality is all about giving you a sense of happy, healthy, calm wellbeing that will keep you engaged and purposeful on the journey of building your personal brand and business success. When our energy is low our willpower plummets. It's harder to concentrate on immediate goals, let alone the bigger picture if we're not looking after ourselves in every dimension. Without reserves of mental, physical and spiritual energy, your journey towards building your personal brand will be way harder than it needs to be.

Looking after yourself also includes self expression. Taking time away from the daily busy-ness and potential grind of work to do what you love to do. Perhaps it's baking cakes or making chocolates – those are my little moments for me — or do you like to read, paint, play sport, visit art galleries, travel, garden, do jigsaw puzzles, play games? Time out doing the things we love is an important act of self expression and love. Taking time for yourself isn't self indulgent nor an optional extra, it's a self love 'must-do'.

Laser-Like Focus

One of the fundamental traits of highly successful people is their ability to deploy laser-like focus on achieving their goals, no matter the distractions, challenges, bumps and bruises along the way. For as long as the goals remain relevant, successful people remain focused. This is especially relevant in building your personal brand as it won't happen overnight, it takes time. It's important that you see the big picture, focus on what you want to achieve and stay the course to achieving your goal. In doing that you'll turbo-boost your effort and you'll see more clearly how to do the work. You'll be amazed and delighted by how much progress you can make and how quickly you start to feel the virtuous circle of achievement and growing self confidence.

Mindset Matters

We all have fears and negative self-beliefs, doubts and criticisms that have taken up residence in our mind. They extinguish our zest for life and our work. They wreck our 'sizzle'. They also double up nicely as excuses. Here's a few of them. Recognise any?

- I'll never be able to do it.
- I can't afford to follow my dream.
- I don't have the skills.
- I might fail and I just couldn't bear it.
- I don't have time.
- They might turn me down.
- I wish I'd done it years ago, now I've lost my chance.

This is by no means a comprehensive list, you can probably add plenty more. We are remarkably good at finding justifications for staying stuck.

Remember you are in control of every thought you think. Choose to fight those that stop you from doing the work towards building your personal brand and achieving your business goals. Don't let your mind undermine you. You can do it.

Be an Eternal Student of You

It would be tempting to only consider your knowledge and your expertise when you are creating your personal brand, but it's through constant learning that you will continue to shape your personal brand and develop relationships with the people who matter. If you want to be a great teacher, you always have to be willing to be a great student.

Even the type of learning that you choose to pursue will infuse your values and your brand identity. Say you were in the wellbeing industry. You might be drawn to learning about different types of meditation and yoga practices, or conversely you might be much more interested in training techniques for reaching peak physical fitness. The types of services and products you offer are more likely to be a hit with your customers if they are a reflection of you. And if you discover that meditation is the 'in thing', you can explore and learn about it from the perspective of someone who would rather be pounding it out in the gym. If, by being open to learning, you discover its benefits then you'll have a strong story to tell others.

Learning will also present opportunities to meet interesting people, many of whom could be a part of your network. You may even end up collaborating with contacts you make, especially in workshop and seminar situations. Always go ready with your elevator pitch –

'what do you do?' – and business cards. Never force the situation, but if interest sparks with someone then it's easy to stay in touch.

A client I was mentoring was asked to attend a conference on Green Britain issues. She was a little wary as her expertise is in writing about health and food, rather than the environment. But she was interested and open both to learning and seeing what the day might bring. There was the usual round robin at the beginning of the day when each delegate briefly said what they do. Kate often gets nervous at this point, worried that she'll stumble or be instantly forgettable. But she decided to keep it really simple and speak up clearly: 'Hi, my name is Kate. I'm a writer with an expertise in writing about food, health and happiness.' She was relieved not to have stumbled, and didn't think any more about it, until the lunch break when two delegates immediately made a bee line for her. The first was the web editor of Sustain, an organisation dedicated to promoting sustainable farming and food practices. She said they always needed content, and especially in the health area. Could they stay in touch? The second was the managing director of one of the largest organic vitamin companies in the UK, who said, 'I just love the idea of food and happiness together, can we talk?'

The organisations and associations linked to your industry will often host seminars and talks. Make space in your diary each month for something linked to learning and your personal brand will naturally take on more shape and definition as your knowledge, expertise and interests expand. Check out your local colleges or universities, festivals and workshops (www.googleforentrepreneurs. com is a great one for start-ups and entrepreneurs).

The Importance of Mentors

Eighty percent of CEOs report having had a mentor at some point during their career. Having a mentor or a coach can be of enormous benefit to you and your personal brand. Often, a mentor will be there to listen as you talk through what's going on in your life and business, and the choices you are weighing up. Other times they might offer a story or experience. A mentor isn't there to push you in any specific direction or give you concrete advice, but they are someone who is simply on your side, someone whose experience and wisdom you admire, and while they aren't there to put pressure on you, somehow you feel accountable and are more likely to go for your goals with their presence in your life.

A mentor can reflect back your strengths and the parts of you that will help you to stand out and be successful. Because you trust their support, they can also challenge you on occasion to consider life beyond your comfort zone. It's much harder when friends and family do this, so finding a mentor through your work, through networking or an organisation you are a member of is a good idea.

It is through being open to new ideas, experiences and learning new skills that you and your personal brand in turn grow. You may discover a new way of doing something in your job or business that turns out to have a huge positive impact on your profits. You may discover new contacts or audience sectors as you attend learning events yourself. If you're willing to learn then there are so many online technologies available to you that will boost your personal brand presence. And simply having an attitude that is keen to learn from others encourages connection and relationships. Curiosity is a very attractive quality.

Mastermind Groups

Have you thought of joining a mastermind group? A mastermind is a group of likeminded people who periodically meet to support each other. Mastermind groups occur in all parts of life, for instance, a book club is a form of mastermind group. Many people participate in business mastermind groups to support and challenge them to achieve their business and personal goals.

Here's a summary of what a mastermind could do to support you as you develop your personal brand and business:

1. **Brainstorming** – leveraging the group's experience.
2. **Accountability** – others who'll hold you to account.
3. **Feedback** – through relationships of trust, offering perspective.
4. **Decision-Making** – getting ideas from others.
5. **Support** – in both the good and difficult times.
6. **Connection** – like minded others on a similar journey.
7. **Confidence** – through learning and engaging with others.
8. **Progression** – motivation to move faster in your business.
9. **Community** – entrepreneurship can be lonely.
10. **Clarity** – others who'll ask questions and challenge you.

11. **Challenge** – you to grow your personal potential.
12. **Introductions** – to people in others' networks.
13. **Profitability** – your business will become more successful.

Summary

As a recovering perfectionist, I know how hard it is to step away from my perfectionist streak and to settle for excellence. Perfectionism can cause us to do nothing, and of course, that achieves nothing. Instead, get on and do the work and accept that as you work on building your personal brand that you'll make mistakes and you'll want to do things better. That's normal. Just get on and do something. Start with passion, and work out exactly want you want to be known for. Can that be your purpose? If so, create a vision that's magnetic for you. Combine all that with a check in on your values. I promise you, in doing that work you'll feel energetic and inspired. Hopefully that will hold you as you get on and do all the other work that's required to create your personal brand too. I love the Shakespeare quote: 'Nothing comes from doing nothing'. Yep, ain't that the truth.

ACTION

You've nearly come to the end of this book on personal branding. What are you going to do first, second and third to begin creating your personal brand? Baby steps are good.

1.

_____

_____

_____

_____

2.

_____

_____

_____

_____

3.

_____

_____

_____

_____

The Queen

> 'I know of no single formula for success. But over the years I have observed that some attributes of leadership are universal and are often about finding ways of encouraging people to combine their efforts, their talents, their insights, their enthusiasm and their inspiration to work together.'

Upon the death her father King George, Princess Elizabeth ascended the throne in February 1952 and was coronated in June 1953. Queen Elizabeth II is Queen of the United Kingdom, Canada, Australia and New Zealand, and is Head of the Commonwealth. Twelve countries have become independent since her accession.

The motto of many British monarchs which Queen Elizabeth exemplifies is: "I serve". While seldom granting interviews, it's apparent that the Queen has a deep sense of religious and civic duty, and abides by her coronation oath. Her workload is enormous, each year undertaking some 400 public engagements, perhaps evidence of the passion and purpose she feels for her role and work, despite her advancing years.

The queen has developed her own strong sense of style, mostly wearing bright colours during her official engagements – she likes to stand out from the crowd. Her style includes dress coats, hats, gloves and a certain type of court shoe and handbag. She's arguably the most photographed woman in the world, and is instantly recognisable.

As a constitutional monarch, Queen Elizabeth must not give her own views on political matters. While her heirs are often more forthright with their views, some argue that her neutrality forms part of her wide appeal.

The queen has continued to modernise 'the Firm' as the Royal family is known. She now takes more financial responsibility for the 'business of royalty' as less money is provided from the British public purse. She was the first member of the royal family to use email and to tweet, and has allowed her work to be enjoyed on many official social media platforms.

The business of the royal family is financially strong, given it's a tourist attraction for millions of visitors across the world. Various palaces and castles are open at selected times of the year for public viewing, and there is much memorabilia on sale to support her coffers and the ongoing renovation and development work that is undertaken at her properties.

The personal wealth of Queen Elizabeth is estimated at over £300 million, although no-one really knows. Her personal wealth excludes many property assets which are held in trust for the future of the British monarchy.

Who knows what the future of the British family will be after her death, but while she lives, Queen Elizabeth will continue to be loved by millions across the world.

CONCLUSION: Now It's Up To You

Remember that at its core, the definition of your personal brand is the feelings that are evoked in others when they hear your name, read your bio or blog, when they see you, talk to you or listen to you speak. It's that two-way connection.

Once you connect the dots between who you are, your purpose and how you can help or provide something special for whom you are targeting, then you will have a personal brand that has confidence shining from within, resulting in attracting more of the right customers, clients and opportunities.

Your personal brand combines your strengths and experience with your passions and your personality so that not only are you someone people can trust but you are someone they relate to, remember after an event, see as an expert in their niche, and who they simply like. When you know who you are and what it is you offer that has value to your audience you can feel confident about communicating your brand using a whole variety of tools that are now available.

When you bring all the elements of personal branding together, you are suddenly able to supercharge your value because when people think of you they think of the unique combination of strengths, experiences and passions that you offer. They feel that they know you, and can therefore trust their perception of you, because everything you are conveying is consistent, is your recognisable style and the best version of you. When people hear about you and do a quick search online, they will find a fantastic professional website and LinkedIn profile, they will notice that everything is current and that you engage with others through your social media platforms, that you offer some great information or insights through your blog or YouTube channel, and that you have some interesting ideas worth spreading.

To succeed, you can't just do a great job, you have to be noticed doing a great job and whatever it is that you are offering to your audience needs to be crystal clear. You want to invoke the response, 'I need that'. However talented, skilled or passionate you are about what you do and what you stand for, if you aren't taking steps to improve your visibility in the right circles and with the right people (quality before quantity), then you'll miss out on opportunities. Remember that it's easier to become known for something specific. You don't have to be all things to all people, in fact that approach will only dilute your personal brand. As you implement the practical tools in this book, always keep focused on what makes you stand out, what are your best attributes that will get you noticed for all the right reasons.

Sometimes, it can be difficult to make time for building your personal brand when you feel stretched enough getting your 'work' done. But instead of thinking of these things as separate and a luxury, know that they are essential to people seeing the value in what you do, that they will lead to not only more work, but more valuable work, to collaborations that may bring more revenue than you could ever have achieved on your own.

I hope you'll begin to put some of these amazing tools available for building your personal brand to work for you. I highly recommend setting aside some dedicated time each day and week so that you can begin to have a consistent and increasingly visible online presence. When people see you, recognise you and feel they know your tone and style then you will start attracting the right people for you and your personal brand. You won't be everyone's cup of tea, no one is, but you will begin to create a network of people who trust and like what you say and what you stand for, and who will come to you when they need that amazing thing it is that you offer. Isn't that what business should be about?

Bonuses

Thank you for reading Branded You. I hope you implement each of the seven pillars in my Personal Brand Star System™.

By visiting and registering at: www.smallbusinesshugesuccess.com/personalbranding you will receive free bonuses which I hope will support you to achieve greater success in building your personal brand and in business.

Bonus One: Customer Avatar Template

In chapter 4 on Positioning, I talked about the importance of identifying your perfect customer. A customer avatar is a composite character who represents real people, where you fully understand their needs, wants and problems. In Bonus One I give you my customer avatar questionnaire and a sample of a customer avatar.

Bonus Two: Résumé Template

In chapter 4 we also talked about the need to write a résumé in business. Résumés must be professional and represent your personal brand. Bonus Two is my résumé template that will help guide you to writing a résumé that best reflects you and your expertise.

Bonus Three: Five Secrets of Savvy Networking

In chapter 6 we look at the importance of platforms, both online and offline. Networking is a key offline platform that most business owners and entrepreneurs must master. There are five key secrets of savvy networking, and they are: 1. Strategic Intent 2. Standing Out 3. Symbiotic Relationships 4. Sales Strategies 5. Systems and Automation. Bonus Three is my free ebook on the Five Secrets of Savvy Networking.

About Adèle McLay

Adèle McLay is passionate about supporting small business owners and entrepreneurs to achieve profitable and sustainable growth, and the success they desire in their businesses.

Adèle is an experienced business adviser, coach and mentor, having advised and consulted to small and large businesses in New Zealand and the United Kingdom for over 25 years. She's also an entrepreneur and investor.

Adèle is an experienced and inspiring keynote speaker, who is regularly asked to speak to business audiences on a range of topics related to business and life, performance and success.

Also From Adèle McLay

Books

Adèle has written another book for Small Business Huge Success™.

Big Profits: 12 Strategies to Substantially Grow YOUR Business Profits (Akitu Press, 2013)

'... *packed full of easy to implement strategies that if applied to any business – big or small – will substantially increase profits*' from foreword by Raymond Aaron, New York Times bestselling author

Bursting with practical steps and real life examples, Big Profits includes all the know-how you need to grow your profits, from addressing your cash flow to managing expenses and targeting your most profitable customers. You'll look at your pricing and implement strategies for finding 'lots more' customers. From outstanding customer service to impeccable financials, Big Profits has it covered for you so that you can strengthen the foundations of your business and upsize your profits.

Business Tips

Adèle presents free business and personal growth tips via social media, YouTube and her email community. To become part of her email community, please visit: www.adelemclay.com

Social Media:

Facebook: Adèle McLay Fan

Instagram: @AdèleMcLay

Twitter: @AdèleMcLay

YouTube: Adèle McLay

Google+:   Adèle McLay

About Small Business Huge Success™

The vision for Small Business Huge Success™ is to inform, inspire and impact business owners and entrepreneurs around the world who want to achieve greater success in their businesses. We offer books, interviews, summits, learning programmes and much more in support of that vision.

If you would like more information on Small Business Huge Success™, please contact:

Small Business Huge Success™
P O Box 56429
London SE3 9UF
Tel: 0044 (0) 203 137 9871
enquiries@smallbusinesshugesuccess.com

Social Media:
Facebook: Small Business Huge Success
Instagram: @Small.Business.Huge.Success